Acquaintance Rape and Sexual Assault Prevention Manual

Acquaintance Rape and Sexual Assault Prevention Manual

Fifth Edition

by Andrea Parrot, Ph.D.

Lp **LEARNING PUBLICATIONS, INC.**
Holmes Beach, Florida

Learning Publications, Inc.
5351 Gulf Drive
P.O. Box 1338
Holmes Beach, FL 34218-1338

Year: 5 4 3 2 1   Printing: 5 4 3 2 1

ISBN 1-55691-076-2

Cover photo by Alan McEvoy

Printed in the United States of America

Contents

Part III – Selected Articles

Part IV – Rape and Sexual Assault Bibliographies

Acknowledgements

This manual was developed over many years. As my work in acquaintance rape prevention evolved, so did my understanding of the issue. The material presented in these pages reflects my background in education, sexuality, sexual assault, and sociology.

I have been fortunate to have had the help of victims of sexual assault, colleagues in the field, and professional technical assistance in the development of this manual. The victims will remain anonymous, but their insights and bravery should be recognized. Steve Allen, M.D., and Tim Marchell provided suggestions regarding content. In addition, the members of the Cornell Coalition Advocating Rape Education provided moral support and content suggestions. Laurie Bechhofer was responsible for the majority of the work on the bibliographies. Susan Lang edited the manual, and Kim Fellows is responsible for the secretarial work. Each of these people contributed to the value of the manual.

I hope our work will be useful to you in your acquaintance rape prevention efforts.

PART I

UNDERSTANDING ACQUAINTANCE RAPE AND SEXUAL ASSAULT

1
INTRODUCTION

Any sexual intercourse without mutual desire is a form of rape. Anyone who is psychologically or physically pressured into sexual contact on any occasion is as much a victim as the person who is attacked on the streets. Our culture exerts multiple pressures both on the people who abuse others sexually and on those who fail to be effectively assertive in avoiding such abuse. The following scenario depicts the complexity of acquaintance rape situations.

Scenario

Betty, a college sophomore, asked Jim out. Jim paid for theater tickets and dinner. They returned to his apartment, which was the scene of their several previous sexual encounters. That night Betty did not want to have sex. In spite of saying "no" repeatedly, Jim forced her to have intercourse.

This is an acquaintance rape, but Betty will not call it rape. Victims of acquaintance rape often cannot accept the fact that they have been raped, and therefore do not define the experience as rape to themselves or to others.

Often acquaintance rape is not recognized as rape because subtle coercion was employed to get the victim to comply with a behavior in which s/he does not want to participate. There are five stages which generally occur in acquaintance rape which involve use of coercion, force, violence or fear for personal safety. The five stages are:

1. Violation of a victim's personal space.

2. The victim does not assert that this behavior is an intrusion of personal space.

3. The assailant escalates the level of violation.

4. The couple ends up in a secluded, vulnerable place.

5. The actual rape occurs.

Acquaintance rape is forced unwanted sexual intercourse in which the attacker and the victim know each other. The victim's story is frequently not believed by others. Date rapes often occur during mutually arranged social engagements; they are the most common type of acquaintance rape on college campuses. Many people would not define such situations as rape because they believe that rape only happens when the attacker is a stranger who uses violence. The acquaintance rape victim must therefore deal with the trauma of the rape without the benefit of psychological support and the outcome is that the rape victim tends to blame herself or himself.

Although laws vary from state to state, generally a situation is legally considered rape is the victim has sex against his or her will and without his or her consent, if the victim is fearful for life or personal safety, or if the attacker uses violence, force, coercion, or the threat of force or violence. Some states consider only forced sexual intercourse rape; others consider other forced sexual behaviors rape as well.

"Acquaintance rape is forced unwanted sexual intercourse in which the attacker and the victim know each other."

According to Professor Mary Koss (1987) who conducted the largest national survey on acquaintance rape of over 6,000 college students on 32 campuses, more than 80% were committed by an acquaintance. This is a problem affecting all types of colleges and universities nationally. Alcohol and drugs frequently contribute to the social conditions which lead to acquaintance rapes. Peer pressure brought to bear on men to have sex, mixed signals given by both men and women, unrealistic expectations, and sexual freedom contribute to the many date rapes which occur on college campuses.

Men who commit acquaintance rape often do not think they have done anything wrong. They believe that a woman never means "no" when she says "no" in a sexual situation. The consequence for the assailant is that he may continue to abuse victim after victim because he thinks this is an acceptable type of behavior (Rapaport and Burkhart, 1984), or he may be arrested for rape.

"Men who commit acquaintance rape often do not think they have done anything wrong."

Professor Barry Burkhart, a leading authority on acquaintance rape, estimates that fewer than 1 in 100 acquaintance rapes are reported to the authorities (Burkhart, 1983). Therefore, most men who commit this crime are never held accountable for it. If the victim reports the incident to an authority, it will most likely be to a counseling agency (Parrot, 1987). If the rape is reported to the police it will probably be dismissed because the authorities believe that a woman must be attacked by a stranger for a rape to occur.

Even if a legal rape charge does not result in a conviction, the lives of both the victim and the alleged assailant will have changed permanently, usually for the worse. They both are likely to feel victimized by the legal system, and they may develop bad reputations as a result of having been involved in an acquaintance rape. Victims often decide to leave college if they come forward to report an incident because there is often tremendous pressure to **drop** the charges. The man charged with rape is often labeled as a rapist even if he is not found guilty.

Distinctions between the various types of rapes and sexual assaults are often subtle, and lead to confusion and disbelief for many people. The definitions below are provided to clear up the confusion regarding rape.

Definitions

Rape – Penis-vagina intercourse against a woman's will and without her consent (this is a legal definition, and varies slightly by state).

Acquaintance Rape – Rape by someone the victim knows.

Date Rape – Rape by someone the victim has been or is dating.

Soft Rape – Coercion used to engage a victim in intercourse against his/her will.

Consentual Sex – Sexual relations with both partners desiring sex.

Simple Rape – Rape without violence or force, with a single assailant or without any other accompanying crime (kidnapping, murder, assault, etc.)

Aggravated Rape – Rape which occurs with more than one assailant or in conjunction with another crime (kidnapping, murder, assault, etc.)

Sexual Assault – A forced sexual act against one's will (men or women may be assaulted according to this definition).

Note: Victims in approximately 10 percent of all sexual assault cases are men.

Most people agree that rape is motivated by a need to overpower, humiliate, and dominate a victim. This is almost always the initial motivation in stranger rape situations. However, the initial motivation in some acquaintance rapes, and many date rapes is sexual. In other words, the offender premeditates sex, not rape. But when the date does not progress to sex the way he had planned, he often becomes angry and takes what he feels he is right. Sex. He does overpower, dominate, and humiliate in the process, and may intend to when he is raping, but that was not his initial motivation. In fact, many date rapists do not think that they did anything wrong.

Acquaintance rape is a very serious problem because it is ubiquitous yet the report rate is very low. Infrequent reporting results in the majority of acquaintance rapists remaining unpunished and free to commit the crime repeatedly. In addition, our legal and social systems are reinforcing this behavior by perpetuating the myths that because many women have rape fantasies, "all women secretly want to be raped," and "if the woman really resisted she could not be raped."

"More than half of the rapes in the United States are acquaintance rapes, ..."

Acquaintance rapes seem to occur most often in private dwellings, such as the victim's or assailant's homes (Parrot and Lynk, 1983). This does not mean that acquaintance rapes can only occur indoors. A high percentage of sexual assaults occur between people who know each other to some degree, such as a friend, co-worker, boyfriend, husband, neighbor, or supervisor. In a situation in which a couple is involved (e.g. on a date), alcohol and loud music are frequently part of the scenario. Loud music seems to be effective in covering the victims noncompliant sounds. Multiple male living units also seem to be frequent sites of sexual assaults.

More than half of the rapes in the United States are acquaintance rapes, but they account for less than half of the incidents reported to police (F.B.I., 1984). This may be because rape by an acquaintance is very difficult to prove, and the victim may feel some responsibility for contributing to the event. This type of rape is often sparked by the assailant's anger if the victim decides not to comply sexually. Pressure not to involve the police, fear of causing an embarrassing situation for themselves in a relatively close community, and fear that their names will not be kept confidential often prevents victims from reporting this type of rape. "Gang rapes" or rape by multiple acquaintances have also been reported on college campuses, although this type of rape is much less frequent than rape by a single acquaintance (Ehrhart and Sandler, 1984; Hughes and Sandler, 1987).

Most rapists are between 15 and 24 years of age (Amir, 1971) which generally puts acquaintance rape victims within the college age range. These potential victims are vulnerable because they have relatively few restrictions and little experience in dealing with the freedom afforded by independent living. College populations appear to be at particularly high risk of becoming involved in an acquaintance rape based on stereotypic attitudes, vulnerability, and social interactions.

Young people seem to be caught in a double bind regarding social behavioral imperatives. Females are supposed to guard their "reputations" (Russell, 1984). Males are expected to have a female sexual partner. Females are supposed to be attractive to males sought after by them, and submissive to them. However, females are not supposed to give sex. Males are confused by the inconsistent messages given by females. At times, verbal and non-verbal messages provide different meanings simultaneously. Females want males to initiate sex to affirm the female's attractiveness. Males are expected to sexually initiate even if they do not want to have sex. Lack of sexual initiation may lead to being labeled "gay" when she reports the events of the evening to her friends. Both members of the couple are "trapped" by societal expectations and mandates.

Both men and women can be victims of rape or sexual assault (depending on the legal definition of the state in which the assault occurred). The F.B.I. estimates that approximately 10 percent of all sexual assaults are on men. Women or men can commit a sexual assault, in either same sex or opposite sex encounters. However, in most rapes the male is the assailant and the female is the victim.

The term woman will usually be used in referring to victims, and the term men will usually be used when referring to offenders so that sentences are less complicated. However, men may also be victims and women may also be offenders. Therefore, gender neutral terms are used whenever possible in this manual, and should also be used whenever possible in leading groups on the topic so that male victims also feel included.

There are a number of prevention strategies for avoiding a potential acquaintance rape situation. Those strategies include trusting instincts, assertive behavior, honest and consistent communication, awareness of surroundings, and remaining in control of the situation. Generally, the greater number of prevention strategies which are employed in a potential rape situation, the greater the likelihood of avoiding the acquaintance rape. There are no "cookbooks" for avoiding sexual assault. Each victim and rapist is different, and each victim needs to make his or her own decisions based on the particular situation.

2
IMPORTANCE OF ACQUAINTANCE RAPE EDUCATION

The reporting of acquaintance rape increased dramatically the first year our acquaintance rape prevention program was introduced on the Cornell University campus (see Table 1), and there has also been a sharp increase in the number of men and women seeking counseling about acquaintance rape. The program is having a significant preventive effect on the campus. Many women will be victims more than once unless they receive counseling or help to prevent repeated victimization. Students who have not been involved in acquaintance rapes are learning ways to avoid the problem. As awareness of the problem increases, incidence should decrease. See "A Model for Acquaintance Rape Prevention Programs on College Campuses."

Table 1
Change in Report Rate for Forced Sex
by An Acquaintance Following the Program

Agency Receiving the Report

Academic Year	Campus Police*	Dean of Students and University Sex Counseling**	Judicial Administrator*
1985-1986	1	12	0
1986-1987	6	33	7

*These figures include those who pressed charges and those who provided information only.

**Psychological Services figures were not available for this analysis.

Table 1 shows that there was approximately a 450% increase in reporting of acquaintance rapes or sexual assaults to campus personnel at Cornell University. I believe that these data are representative of greater reporting rather than increased incidence of acquaintance rape, because approximately one-sixth of the reports were of events which took place before 1986. This means students are seeking help to recover from their rapes at a much greater rate than ever before. Between 1975 and 1985, there were fewer than 10 acquaintance rapes in total reported on this campus. In the 1986-87 academic year, 46 acquaintance rapes were reported. We can not help students deal with the trauma associated with acquaintance rapes and sexual assaults if they do not come forward.

The best way to avoid the emotional devastation associated with acquaintance rape is to prevent it.

Both men and women stand to benefit from the reduction of the acquaintance rape problem because male/female relationships will be improved; women will be less fearful of men; there will be fewer repeat victims; and men will be less likely to commit acquaintance rape.

3

THE ROLE OF SEX ROLE SOCIALIZATION IN FORCED SEX SITUATIONS

Forced intercourse and rape are synonyms, yet most people do not generally use the terms interchangeably. Many acquaintance rape victims feel that they were forced to have intercourse, but deny that they were raped. This discrepancy stems from our socialization and cultural standards, which lead to the common notion that rape only happens when a stranger jumps out of the bushes.

Vulnerability to Forced Sex

Our cultural view of femininity often includes traits such as submissiveness, passivity, and weakness. These characteristics make women vulnerable to rape (Russell, 1975). There is also an expectation that a woman must be associated with a boyfriend, male lover, or husband to be successful, regardless of the success she has achieved in her career. If traditional female behaviors are operative in a rape situation, the woman is often seen as having "contributed" to the rape. If a woman behaves submissively toward the man, as she has been trained to act, then the sexual experience will often not be viewed as rape (Russell, 1975). Since she did not resist, the event is not viewed in her mind as rape. Few women are encouraged to develop the strength necessary to resist a man. Most women, in fact, are discouraged from learning how to fight because fighting and anger are considered "unladylike" (Russell, 1975).

Other components of traditional female behavior include kindness, compassion, patience, acceptance, and dependence. Women are expected to take primary responsibility for solving problems in their relationships with men. A woman may not want to appear rude or suspicious of her date or male companions and many behave in ways to protect a man's ego at the expense of protecting herself.

"Females today are being placed in dating situations that require sophisticated decision making capabilities, insight into human behavior, and an intricate understanding of sexual behavior."

Women who reject traditional patterns of feminine behavior are also vulnerable to rape because they are more likely to take risks (Russell, 1984). They are more likely to hitchhike, walk home alone at night, or live alone. The women's movement has been partly responsible for exposing acquaintance rape as a crime and changing rape laws, but it has also given some women a false sense of security.

Liberal women may believe that they are no longer bound by rigid traditional expectations. Yet, many people still operate under the notion that women should behave in traditional ways, and any variation from those patterns indicates that a woman was "asking for rape."

Females today are being placed in dating situations that require sophisticated decision making capabilities, insight into human behavior, and an intricate understanding of sexual behavior. These dating situations may occur several years earlier for teens than they did for their parents. A thirteen-year-old may be faced with making decisions about intercourse, even if she is not dating. Group activities, such as parties, often include some time when members of the group may have intimate private time with others. In addition, with so many parents working, teens may use their parents' home after school for intimate interactions.

If rape occurs in an acquaintance or dating relationship where the female has asked the male to her home, or has consented to petting prior to the incident, the female is frequently seen as wholly or partially responsible. "But it does not follow that because a woman engages in sexual 'foreplay' she has acquiesced to intercourse, although the very notion of 'foreplay' assumes it is preliminary to penetration" (Russell, 1975, p. 271). A first year college student in Alabama explains his expectation for intercourse after foreplay:

> I think I could be provoked enough to rape a girl. But it would be her fault for provoking me. She'd have to push me pretty hard. If I was on a date and she grabbed my dick, I could lose control. If she wants to touch it she should want it. I'm not saying it's okay to do, but if a woman grabs you, you **feel** like doing it (Beneke, 1982, p. 54).

This passage depicts the way some men view sexual interactions. Men tend to be penetration oriented, while women more often desire sex which does not culminate in penetration (Hite, 1976, 1981).

Rape will not stop until offenders stop raping. Since most offenders are male, greater emphasis must be placed on educating men to take responsibility to control their sexual urges and to re-examine the feelings that men are better than women.

Some men think that their sexual urges or peer pressure require them to have sex regardless of the wishes of their partners. They may not claim responsibility for their actions if their penises' urge them to have sex. In fact, some men in our culture give their penises proper names of their own, such as Henry, George, or Big Tom. In this case the personification of the penis allows the man to blame the forced sex on Big Tom, because he has given Big Tom a personality and intellect of his own. Some men say that "the little head did the thinking for the big head," meaning that the penis' head controlled its actions. Men must learn that they control their penises, not vice versa.

The other major issue which allows men to force sex on their partners, regardless of their partners wishes is the notion of superiority. If a man thinks he is better than women, he is likely to think that he can do what he wants to women, because his needs are more important. People generally do not exploit their equals, but are more likely to exploit others who they feel are inferior to them. If men viewed women as equals, heterosexual acquaintance rape would probably diminish significantly.

Attitudes Toward Forced Sex

UCLA researchers asked teenagers under what circumstances is it acceptable for a male to hold a female down and force intercourse on her. More than half of the males in the survey responded that it was acceptable if she led him on, or if she said she was going to have sex with him and then changed her mind (Giarrusso, Johnson, Goodchilds, Zellman, 1979). More than a third of the men considered forced sex acceptable if he spent a lot of money on her, had been dating her for a long time, has been permitted to touch her above the waist, is so turned on that he thinks he can't stop, or if she is stoned or drunk (Giarrusso, et al., 1979).

Some females in the UCLA study also felt that it is acceptable for a man to force a woman to have sex. Almost one third of the females in the study thought that forced sex was acceptable if they had dated a long time (32%), if she says she is going to have sex with him and then changes her mind (31%), if she let him touch her above the waist (28%), and if she "led him on" (27%) (Giarruso, 1979). From these findings it is clear that women, too, need to reconsider justification for rape.

The most common type of force or coercion used to force a woman to have intercourse in college populations is a situation in which the woman is pressured with arguments (Parrot, 1985). Neil Malamuth (1981) studied college aged men regarding their proclivity to rape and about 35% of the men studied indicated

"If men viewed women as equals, heterosexual acquaintance rape would probably diminish significantly."

that they would be likely to rape if they could be assured of not being caught. Although many men may be in situations which could lead to acquaintance rape, only about 5% report actually committing rape (Koss et al., 1987).

In instances of acquaintance rape, blaming the victim is a cultural norm which prevents the assailant and the victim from believing that the man is to blame. Both believe she contributed to the circumstances that led to the rape. Many people believe that women invite rape by being flirtatious (MacDonald, 1971; Amir, 1971; Schiff, 1973, cited in Katz and Mazur 1979).

Common Factors

Alcohol (Russell, 1984; Rada, 1975) and loud music (Parrot and Link, 1983) are common factors in acquaintance rape situations. Both are usually present at college parties and bars. The most common location for forced intercourse following coercion is a home or apartment. When actual force is employed, the most common locations are in dorms, apartments, fraternities, and outside. Single sex living units (such as all-male dorms or fraternity houses) are also likely settings because peer pressure is often associated with irresponsible male behavior (Russell, 1984). Many young men in all-male living units are noisy, rowdy, and silly; they act immaturely, drink excessively, and play crude jokes on others (Walters, McKellar, Lipton, Karme, 1981).

Repeat Victimization Patterns

Many women feel passive after they have been victims of rape or sexual assault. "Having been overcome by a rapist leaves a feeling of having been conquered" (Russell, 1984, p. 162). Virgins who have been raped are especially vulnerable to passivity and diminished self-esteem, which may explain why women who are victimized when young are more likely to be victims of repeat sexual assaults. Socialized female behavior patterns coupled with loss of self-esteem may account for a recurring cycle of victimization. A woman may feel that she needs a man, put herself into a vulnerable situation to be with one, not feel important enough to ask him to take her into account, and finally become violated sexually.

Women are most vulnerable to forced intercourse in the late teen years. They remain at particular risk during their first year, but the number of assaults decreases as they pass through college. Women who are victims of multiple forced sexual assaults most likely have a partner who lies to obtain sex.

A woman is less likely to define forced intercourse as rape if she knows the man well. Therefore, the better a woman knows her assailant, the less likely she is to call a forced sex situation "rape." The assailant may be more likely to commit rape again if he gets away with it the first time, and his first victim may become his victim again. He may even think that she did not report the rape because she liked the experience.

If the problem of acquaintance rape is to decrease among young women, there must be a change in our socializing of young males and females, and an interruption of this pattern of early victimization.

4
PATTERNS ASSOCIATED WITH ACQUAINTANCE RAPE

Many forced sex events occur in places where the victim should be able to feel safe, such as in her own home or the home of the offender. Once a couple is in the setting in which the forced sex will occur, the man is likely to lie or threaten the woman to get her to comply with his wishes for sex. How can a woman protect herself from becoming a victim of forced sex with someone she knows and possibly trusts? The most effective preventive strategy is to avoid a vulnerable situation. Once in a potential acquaintance rape situation, however, assertive actions or multiple avoidance strategies are most effective. (Bart, 1981).

Settings and Circumstances in which Forced Sex Occurs

The vast majority of rapes occur in a private dwelling or other private property (Bancroft, et al., 1982). Forty percent of all reported rapes occur in a home (Martinez, 1983). Bart (1981) reported that women who were raped were most often assaulted in their home. Although most acquaintance rapes occur indoors within a private dwelling, acquaintance rape may happen anywhere. According to Beherns (1981), there are three settings or circumstances in which acquaintance rapes are most likely to occur.

1. **On a date:** Couples are less likely to enter either of their apartments on a first date because social defenses are usually highest at this time. Acquaintance rape, therefore, is more likely to occur on a second or third date.

2. **After a chance meeting:** A disco, singles bar or party often sets the stage for an acquaintance rape. Such situations may lead to miscommunication in which she may be thinking "coffee," while he may be thinking "sex."

3. **In the neighborhood:** The rapist may be an employee of the local store, a rebuffed neighbor, ex-boyfriend, or other neighborhood member.

A high percentage of sexual assaults occur between people who know each other. Interactions with a boyfriend's friend, co-worker, uncle, husband's boss, husband, or neighbor all may lead to the development of potentially dangerous and undeserved trust.

Coercion, Force, and Violence used in Acquaintance Rape or Sexual Assault

Acquaintance rape is frequently thought to lack the real elements of rape because of the voluntary association between the victim and the assailant. This type of assault, therefore, is often not recognized as rape. In fact, only one in five reported rapes is believed by the police, general public, jurors, or judges because many are acquaintance rapes which are often not perceived as rape (Zellman et al., 1979). The stronger the force used and the weaker the relationship between the victim and the assailant, the more likely the rape will be labeled as rape (Zellman et al., 1979). When physical force is used, the experience is more often labeled rape. When threats or verbal coercive behavior is used, the experience is usually not identified as rape. Even when violence is used on the victim, the experience is frequently not defined as rape if the victim and assailant are dating (Zellman et al., 1979).

Because men have much more experience with physical force than women, men do not need weapons to intimidate women (Barrett, 1982). Some men feel entitled to coercive sex and feel that the woman's feelings about sex are less important. This refers specifically to the situation in which a woman says "no" but the man interprets her to mean "yes" or "maybe."

In a 1981 study at Kent State, 27 percent of the men had used emotional or physical force when their dates were unwilling to engage in sexual relations, while 43 percent of the men admitted to using violence to obtain sex (Koss & Oros, 1981). In addition, 24 percent of the women and 7 percent of the men reported having been threatened or forced to have sexual relations (Koss et al., 1981).

According to another study, almost all the male undergraduates asked felt it was acceptable for a woman to ask directly for a date, drop hints, or wait to be asked for a date, providing the man liked the woman (Muehlenhard and McFall, 1981). The college men were then given three descriptions of dates between a heterosexual couple which varied in respect to who initiated the date, where the couple went, and who paid. Results showed that men rated intercourse against the woman's wishes as significantly more justifiable when 1) the woman initiated the date, 2) the couple went to the man's apartment rather than to the movies or a religious function, and 3) when the man paid the expenses for the evening (Muehlenhard and McFall, 1981). It appears that a woman's assertive actions, therefore, may be considered justification for rape. It is important to consider how assertive behavior may be misinterpreted by men, rather than to conclude that women should avoid assertive requests.

Victimization Patterns

The special terror of rape by a date or acquaintance stems from the fact that there is really no protection against it, no way to know that a friendly invitation to dinner may lead to something more. The "nice" man who takes his date home may decide he wants sex and may take it, even if it means violence to some degree. There is no way to predict when an acquaintance rape will occur.

A current sexual relationship between a potential victim and assailant seems a significant factor influencing the likelihood of acquaintance rape. In fact, when a couple has engaged in sexual intercourse in the past, rape is almost never avoided after the voluntary intercourse (Bart, 1981, 1985). An attack will likely culminate in rape when the victim knows the offender, when the only "defense" strategy used is talking or pleading, when the assault takes place in the woman's home, when the woman's primary concern is with not being killed or mutilated, and when the assailant uses threat or force (Bart, 1981). Women are more likely to avoid rape when they are attacked by strangers, when they use multiple strategies, when the assault occurs outside, and when the primary concern is to avoid rape.

A victim's lack of awareness may be viewed by the assailant as inviting coercive behavior. Women are usually not prepared for acquaintance rape, and are not aware of cues they are giving which may be misinterpreted. Most women are aware of potential stranger rape situations and have been warned to avoid dark alleys, hitchhiking, and answering doorbells without knowing the identity of the caller. Women also often think that rape by an acquaintance only happens to others, and are usually unaware of settings that are frequently associated with acquaintance rapes. Since women are never able to tell which men may be potential rapists, women should be cautious at all times.

If a woman has reached adulthood without having been a victim of acquaintance rape or sexual assault, her chances of avoiding one are increasingly good. Conversely, if a young woman has been a victim of sexual assault early in her teen

"The special terror of rape by a date or acquaintance stems from the fact that there is really no protection against it, no way to know that a friendly invitation to dinner may lead to something more."

years, she is more likely to be in similar situations in the future (Parrot and Lynk, 1983).

The two most common forms of coercion used by men are the threats of ending the relationship and arguing that sex should be performed (Parrot et al., 1983). Force, however, seems the most successful strategy to get the victim to comply with the assailant's wishes.

Women who have had assertiveness and self defense training are correlated with avoiding acquaintance rape situations (Parrot et al., 1983). This may be because these women feel confident that they can handle themselves in most difficult situations. Such confidence and related skills may make women less vulnerable to exploitation; the actual employment of self defense skills does not seem as important as simply the possession of the skill.

Young men and women must develop an understanding of relationships, individual rights, and appropriate behavior. Young women must also avoid experiencing a self-perpetuating pattern of sexual assault involvement. Both men and women must be involved in efforts to prevent acquaintance rape, since both are affected by the event of forced sex by acquaintances.

5

RELATIONSHIP BETWEEN SELF ESTEEM, LOCUS OF CONTROL, AND ACQUAINTANCE RAPE

Melanie, a college sophomore, agreed to go to a fraternity party with Julie, a friend of hers, because Julie didn't want to go alone. Julie had a car and planned to drive the 10 miles to the fraternity house. Melanie never really liked fraternity parties, but went because Julie was her friend and had asked her.

Once at the party, they squeezed into the living room where music by Prince was blasting and about 150 people were dancing and talking. To be heard, people had to be within a few inches of each other. A tremendous amount of beer was being served, and the lights were low. Melanie was not really having a good time at the start of the evening because she was separated from Julie and had not met anyone interesting. She was sure it was because she was so plain. Melanie stayed, hoping things would get better, and because Julie looked like she was having a good time.

After a half hour by herself, Jeff, one of the brothers who lived in the house, started to talk to Melanie. She didn't like him at first, but continued to talk to him because he was paying attention to her and he kept her beer glass filled. They danced and talked. Jeff suggested that they go into the less crowded dining room because he was getting hoarse from yelling loud enough for Melanie to hear him over the music. They escaped into the dining room and Melanie could no longer see Julie.

Melanie drank more than she could handle and lost track of time. When she wanted to go look for Julie, she had trouble breaking into Jeff's dull monologue about the lacrosse team. After what seemed like an eternity, she finally slipped from Jeff to look for Julie, but was told by one of the brothers that Julie had left. Melanie had no way to get home. Jeff offered to let Melanie sleep in his room since his roommate was away for the weekend. Melanie accepted reluctantly, but insisted that Jeff promise that they would sleep in separate beds. He promised.

When they got to Jeff's room, they could still hear the music. Jeff started to kiss Melanie and unbutton her blouse. Melanie whispered "no" while allowing Jeff to continue. Jeff persisted. Melanie discovered that she was getting sexually excited at Jeff's skillful touch and by thinking that she was exciting Jeff. Melanie allowed him to continue, thinking that she would stop him before intercourse. Jeff continued to undress Melanie and himself. When Melanie reached the point where she really wanted him to stop, she said "no" again a little louder, but she did not physically resist him. He didn't seem to believe that she wanted him to stop. He assured her that they could sleep in separate beds "in a little while." She was sure he would honor her request to stop if she really insisted. When Melanie began to struggle Jeff became even more excited, and he entered her. He assumed Melanie really wanted sex too, but she wasn't willing to say so because "good girls" aren't supposed to admit that they want sex. Jeff thought he was really doing Melanie a favor by giving her what she wanted (intercourse) without making her take the responsibility. After he ejaculated, he kept his promise and moved into his own bed to sleep. Jeff assumed that Melanie enjoyed the experience as much as he did.

This was an acquaintance rape because Melanie knew Jeff, did not want to have intercourse, but did so against her will.

The Role of Self-Esteem

Melanie's very low self-esteem was a significant factor in her date rape. Melanie's feeling of valuelessness contributed to her going to a party she really didn't want to go to, and to her staying when she wasn't having a good time, because she thought that was what Julie wanted. She stayed with Jeff, and had trouble interrupting him to look for Julie because she didn't want him to think she was rude. Melanie allowed Jeff to become sexual with her even though she didn't want him to because she felt it was her fault that **she** got him excited. She wasn't consistent in explaining her intentions when she wanted him to stop (she whispered "no" while allowing him to continue).

Exploitation (in both sexual and non-sexual arenas) is a common problem for those with low self-esteem because they have difficulty asserting themselves. They may feel they do not have a right to ask for what they want and, therefore, do not make assertive requests. Patterns of low self-esteem and lack of assertiveness often stem from early childhood. In our culture, masculinity is equated with high self-esteem and positive feelings about oneself (Thomas, 1983). Since few women are socialized to behave in a masculine manner, many women have lower self-esteem than many men.

People, especially teenagers, tend to develop notions of how valuable they are based on how others perceive them. A major task of adolescence is to develop a cohesive personal identity (Erikson, 1968). Elkind (1967) believes that adolescents experience a heightened self-consciousness and sensitivity to others' impressions as they develop inferential skills. Therefore, if teenagers are repeatedly told that they are "no good," "worthless," or that they are not able "to do anything right," they may not feel important enough to ask for what they want. Low self-esteem also makes it difficult for them to reject overtures by others who they view as more important (such as a popular 16-year old boy asking a 15-year old girl, "Do you want a beer?"). This is especially true if a person believes the only way

"Exploitation (in both sexual and non-sexual arenas) is a common problem for those with low self-esteem because they have difficulty asserting themselves."

to increase his or her value within the peer group is to be associated with someone of greater value. The teen who perceives him or herself as being of little value may want to be associated with the most popular teen to gain entrance to the "in group."

This behavior is also seen in adolescence when a young woman with low self-esteem is going out with someone very popular, such as the captain of the football team. She may not want to have sex with him, but she is afraid that if she says "no" she will lose him and that her value will be lessened if she is no longer associated with him. If he tells her that "everyone else is having sex, and something is wrong with people who don't," she may comply because she thinks he knows more than she does and that she must have sex with him to keep him.

Parents can make significant contributions to the positive or negative self-esteem of their children develop. It is imperative that parents carefully consider comments to their children which may impact on the development of self image. Gecas (1972) and Thomas and others, (1974) report that the main effect of positive interactions with parents is the confirmation in the children's minds that they are competent, effective, and worthwhile individuals. Overall, parents tend to be more influential in the development of self-esteem of their children than are peers; this is especially true for females (Openshaw, Thomas, and Rollings, 1984). Parents who induce (discuss to the point of mutual agreement) rather than coerce (force compliance with threats) nurture higher self esteem in their children. Adolescents who report feeling coerced experience feelings of inadequacy, inferiority, and lack of self-confidence (Openshaw, et al., 1984). Reflected appraisal (viewing self as a mirror image of the way others do) by opposite sex parents may be more instrumental in the development of a child's self-esteem than modeling of the same sex parental behavior (Openshaw, et al., 1984).

Young adolescents assume that others' opinions of them are more accurate than their opinions of themselves. If there is an incongruity between others' and their own perceptions, the adolescent will usually believe he or she is in error (Rosenbery, 1979). If minority group (female, black, hispanic, etc.) children's significant others hold favorable attitudes toward them, they are likely to have high self-esteem (Louden, 1977). This is more true for younger teens since adolescents generally develop increasingly accurate perceptions of themselves as they grow older (Herzberger, Dix, Erlebacher, Ginsberg, 1981).

Those with low self esteem generally feel that they are worthless and ineffectual much of the time. They feel powerless and impotent at controlling their environment, and, therefore, feel that the environment is externally controlled. They often believe that their efforts never do any good to change their lives for the better. They accept responsibility only for their failures and ignore or discount their contribution to success (Antaki & Brewin, 1982). Those with high self-esteem, on the other hand, tend to accept responsibility for successes and almost ignore or discount responsibility for failures.

Locus of Control

Individuals may perceive events in their lives as controlled **externally** (by others or circumstances) and out of their power, or **internally** by one's own actions and, therefore, within one's power. Stephens (1973) reports that parental warmth, attentiveness, relaxedness, and a high quality parent-child relationship are positively correlated with children who have **internal** perceptions of the events around them. Parental involvement, supportiveness, and disciplinary consistency are major determinants for children to develop perceptions that they have significant control over their environments (Rotter, 1966).

Parents can help their child realize that children really do have some control over the events in their lives. For example, parents can explain that a child probably failed a test because he or she did not study, not because the teacher wrote a bad test. If the child believed that he or she could have changed the outcome of the event, the control would be viewed as **internal**. If the child believed that his or her test scores are not positively correlated with the amount of studying done but are dependent on how good the test is, the control is viewed as **external**. If a child is treated badly by other children due to racial prejudice, the child has very little control over his or her treatment, and

control is viewed as **external**. Perceptive individuals may view some elements in their lives as internally controlled (such as achieving good grades in school), while viewing others as externally controlled (such as droughts causing world hunger).

Parents can be helpful by pointing out which events are externally controlled and which are internally controlled. This ultimately helps a child learn the difference. Whether people believe that they are in control of situations and can determine their own fates within limits is of critical importance to the way they cope with stress and engage in challenges (Lefcourt, 1976).

"Individuals who believe they can make a difference in the social events of their lives, may be more likely to withstand the social pressures in an acquaintance rape situation."

"Internals" as compared with "externals" have better interpersonal relationships, are more assertive, earn more respect from others, and are more resistant to the influence of others. Internals are also better emotionally adjusted, have higher self-esteem, a better sense of humor, less anxiety and depression, less severe psychiatric diagnoses, and report greater life satisfaction and contentment (Crandall and Crandall, 1983).

Individuals who believe they can make a difference in the social events of their lives, may be more likely to withstand the social pressures in an acquaintance rape situation. But, if the individual has an external locus of control regarding social events, i.e., believes that he or she has little or no control over social events, acquaintance rape victimization is more likely because he or she may believe that nothing within his or her control will help prevent the rape.

Relationship of Locus of Control and Self Esteem to Acquaintance Rape

The belief that one can control the events in life may be more important than if one truly can. If a woman is in a situation which has the potential for turning into an acquaintance rape, and she believes that her actions will not change the "inevitable" outcome, she will probably not even attempt to change the situation.

There are many times in Melanie's scenario when Melanie could have taken control of the situation. Perhaps she behaved as she did because she did not know what else to do, did not feel she had a right to act differently, or felt that no matter what she did, she could not change the outcome of the evening.

In reality, Melanie had many options that could have altered the outcome of the scenario. She could have stayed home. She could have taken cab fare, arranged with Julie where to meet and when to go home, or made sure there was another ride available. Earlier in the evening when Melanie was not having a good time, she could have asked Julie to take her home. She could have stayed where she could see Julie. She could have checked to see if anyone else at the party was going in the direction of her home. If she really had no way home, she could have slept on the sofa in the fraternity house. Most importantly, she could have been emphatically clear when she wanted Jeff to stop his sexual advances. She could have screamed to attract attention when Jeff ignored her request to stop. She could have tried to defend herself.

Neither Melanie's behavior or her failure to act in a certain way make Melanie responsible for the rape. Although Jeff is responsible for this crime Melanie did put herself in a vulnerable situation in which an acquaintance rape is more likely. Jeff controlled the event.

Why did Melanie not consider any of the possible alternative courses of action? Could her lack of initiative be due to low self esteem or to viewing the world as externally controlled? Melanie was unwilling or unable to pursue an alternative. Perhaps she felt that she did not have the right to ask for what she wanted, or that she wasn't worth the consideration of others. Perhaps she just assumed that assertive behaviors wouldn't do any good. After all, she did tell Jeff "no," and he ignored her request.

If adolescents feel they do not have the right or ability to control their environment to meet their needs, they are unlikely to employ acquaintance rape prevention strategies. Perhaps we should work toward attempting to improve their self-esteem and help them see that their actions can and do influence their lives.

The earliest logical intervention point is with parents, to help them socialize their children to have high self esteem and to view the world with an internal locus of control.

6
PARENTS' ROLE IN ACQUAINTANCE RAPE PREVENTION

The possibility of acquaintance rape or sexual assault of children may be more frightening to parents than to their children (no matter how old the children). Parental fear may be due, in part, to the awareness that adults know of the realities of sexual assaults and to the recognition that parents cannot ensure protection for their children in all situations.

Give Children Freedom To Learn

Some parents want to spare their children the trauma of "growing pains." To achieve this, many impose restrictions such as curfews or not allowing teens to date until later in high school as ways to keep teens from encountering serious problems. These parental actions, however, may actually be depriving them of or postponing valuable learning experiences. The result may be more severe problems when the teen leaves home than would have occurred had he or she been given the freedom to learn from minor mistakes while living at home.

Parents have the unique opportunity to help their children learn to assess situations, make decisions, and act appropriately by giving the child enough freedom to encounter some difficult social situations. Social learning theory suggests that (Muuss, 1975) if teens have practice making age-appropriate decisions and correcting mistakes, they will improve these skills as they get older. With practice during adolescence they will be able to handle problems of adulthood better. Lewin (1936) suggested that adolescent difficulties can be minimized by equalizing the status between adolescents and adults. If adolescents are treated like adults, they are more apt to act like adults.

"Parents have the unique opportunity to help their children learn to assess situations, make decisions, and act appropriately by giving the child enough freedom to encounter some difficult social situations."

Friedenberg (1959) postulated that social conflict leads to stress and strain, and ultimately to maturity. Psychological maturity stems from being challenged, overcoming obstacles of crisis, and conquering meaningful frustration. Few teens are capable of handling the problems of adolescence well without the guidance of a caring and concerned adult.

These theories suggest that conflict is necessary for development of emotional maturity. Treating adolescents with increasing freedom as they approach adulthood will encourage them to act as adults. Without this maturity, adolescents are at a tremendous disadvantage in facing and solving the traumas encountered in independent living.

As the social pressures of society become more complex, and adolescents face new social and legal freedoms, they are at risk of becoming involved in difficult situations without the skills and maturity necessary to avoid them. Assertiveness, positive self esteem, and good communication patterns are necessary tools to develop adult maturity.

Model Assertiveness

Assertiveness is one of the important skills necessary to effectively cope with the problems encountered in adolescence and adulthood. Aggression or passivity are often employed in difficult situations, yet the results are frequently less than satisfactory. Assertiveness allows one to meet his or her needs without violating the needs of others in the process. For example, asking someone who is smoking a cigarette in a non-ventilated place to smoke where there is adequate ventilation is an assertive request. Children learn many of their behavior patterns from their parents or guardians (for convenience the term "parent" will imply both). If parents behave unassertively, children are likely to behave unassertively as well.

Many women have been reinforced for being unassertive. Being polite, passive, giving, and willing to sacrifice for the needs of others are usual female behaviors that are practiced at the expense of the unassertive person. Assertive behaviors allow women to ask for what they need, thereby decreasing their risk of putting themselves in vulnerable situations. Women must examine and reevaluate learned non-assertive behaviors if assertiveness is the goal. Assertiveness exhibited by women is important, but acceptance of these assertive requests must be evident to children as well. If the mother makes an assertive request but the father ignores it or "puts her down" for the request, children will probably not learn to model positive assertiveness.

Nurture Positive Self Esteem

People tend to develop notions of how valuable they are based on the reflection of how others see them. Therefore, if children are repeatedly told that they are "no good," or "worthless," or that they are not able "to do anything right," they will not feel important enough to ask for what they want.

Poor self esteem also makes it difficult to reject overtures by peers who are viewed as more important (such as "do you want to play doctor?"). This is especially true if a person believes the only way to increase his or her value within the peer group is to be associated with someone of greater value. The child of perceived lesser value will want to play with the most popular child on the block to gain entrance to the "in group."

Parents often make significant contributions to the positive or negative self esteem their children develop. It is imperative that parents carefully consider their comments to children which may impact on the development of self image (for more on developing a child's positive self esteem, refer to Chapters E and G).

Communicate Openly About Sex

One clear message parents give that contributes to negative self esteem is referring to parts of the body as "bad" or "dirty." This message is conveyed when the genitals, for example, are referred to as "unmentionables," "down there," or by a strange term which has a negative connotation (such as "prick" for penis). Seldom do parents say that the child has a "beautiful vulva" or a "lovely penis" the way many speak about "beautiful eyes," or a "beautiful smile."

Children will not be able to communicate accurately about sex if they do not know the correct terms for body parts or sexual behaviors. Children will ask questions about all topics which are considered acceptable. If sex is an acceptable and normal topic in the home, children are likely to discuss it with their parents and each other. This not only provides parents with the opportunity to give accurate information, but also conveys their values about sex to their children. If sex is not discussed at home, children have to guess how their parents feel about it.

Another advantage of open communication about sex is that children will be more apt to discuss the topic with their peers. Young people often hear inaccurate messages about sex (such as "everybody is doing it"). Such inaccuracies could be corrected by an informed teen if sex were considered an acceptable topic at home and if accurate information was obtained from the parents. If teens learn at home that discussing sex is acceptable, they may be willing to convey the information they have learned from their parents.

If an acquaintance rape does occur, the victim may feel less inhibited about going to her parents for help if a good communication pattern had been previously established. For the lines of communication to be open when the child really needs to talk about a sexual problem in later life, good communication patterns must begin in early life.

Sexual problems may begin in preadolescence and continue for the remainder of life. Rate of breast or penis development, concerns about nocturnal emissions, premature ejaculation, or lack of menstruation are common topics of concern for teenagers and their parents. Teens are often too embarrassed to discuss these topics with their parents unless the patterns of sexual communication have been established earlier in life. During adolescence, there are too many other stresses in the parent/child relationship to effectively establish good sexual communication patterns. The later in life sexual communication is established, the more difficult the task, but it is better to start sexual communication late than not at all.

Help Children Learn From Mild Failure Experiences

Adolescents are often awkward at sexual communication and interactions, and they usually do not view parents as a resource for help when they have a social/sexual problem. If parents are viewed as allies, however, rather than dictators, they can provide practice for children to correct problems caused by mistakes in social situations. Without practice at responding to social failure with the parent available as a problem solving resource, the teen may not develop the skills necessary to deal with similar experiences once away from home.

Many parents assume an authoritarian role to protect their children from potentially embarrassing or harmful situations. For example, wasting money on mail order record clubs, wearing an inappropriate outfit to a social event, being stuck at a school dance without a way to get home, going to a party where alcohol will be served, or becoming pregnant at age 16 are situations most parents want their children to avoid. Parents sometimes impose rigid rules or curfews without explaining their reasoning, or without taking the adolescent's need for autonomy into consideration. A curfew will only prevent pregnancies which result from late night intercourse. It will not prevent intercourse earlier in the afternoon after school. The more likely result of overly strict regulations will be resentment on the part of the teenager for being treated like a child.

Teens are more likely to reflect the values of their parents if they have internalized their parents' values. This will most likely happen if parents are consistent in acting and speaking about these values. Inconsistencies, for example, would be telling children that they should not be violent, but spanking children as a means of discipline; or telling children they should not cheat or steal, but then cheating on income taxes. Parents can also encourage internalized parental values by explaining why they have decided to do something, rather than saying, "do it because I am your mother, and I told you to do it."

"Very strict parents may be doing more harm than good."

Very strict parents may be doing more harm than good. A daughter may lie to give her parents the answer they want. Non-communication about important social issues can have devastating results, especially when the teen does not learn important problem solving and decision making techniques in social situations from parents. In addition, if the teen has not encountered mild failure experiences with the parent available as a guide to problem solving, they may have trouble doing so once they leave home.

A more helpful approach would be for parents to be available to their children when a problem arises, and to guide the adolescent through the problem solving process without solving the problem for him or her (Adams, Fay, Loren-Martin, 1984). Discussing such failure experiences, parents can enhance positive communication patterns and prepare the teen to better deal with social interactions encountered in an independent or college situation.

If advice is given before it is sought, though, the teen may resent the parental involvement, and may not have the opportunity to learn from his or her mistake. For example, if a teenager does not have the desired date for the prom because of playing "hard to get," parents may want to intervene to help the teen avoid the pain of not getting the desired date. Teens could benefit from their parents maturity, knowledge, and skills in situations like this, once they realize that they have made a mistake, and are willing to seek parental advice to solve the problem. The parental role here would be to help the adolescent understand why the situation evolved rather than solving the problem for him or her.

If a teenage woman had agreed to a date with someone she does not want to date, and she is unsure of how to get out of the situation, she may seek help from the parent. The most important role for parents in this case is to help her understand why she is in the situation, not to solve the problem for her. She may have been unassertive in expressing her desires because she does not know how to be assertive, or because she is not sure what she really wants. She needs to learn assertive behaviors, and must be willing to use them. The more practice she gets in behaving assertively, the easier it will become for her to be assertive. She must also be encouraged to think about what she really wants before she makes a decision. If she agreed to go out with this young man because she was not sure what she wanted and she did not want to hurt his feelings, then she must be encouraged to put off giving answers until she is sure of what she wants.

A very important parental task is to give her permission to reverse a decision if she has changed her mind. But she must learn to make her intentions clear, rather than giving a mixed message. For example, she should be willing to say "I feel uncomfortable about dating you, so I will not be able to spend time with you in the future, I hope this didn't inconvenience you." She should not give him an inconsistent or mixed message such as "I am sorry I won't be able to go out with you this weekend, but I am not feeling well, maybe we can do it another time."

Once teenagers leave home and begin to work or enter college, they should be armed with problem solving and decision making skills, self confidence, the ability to assess social situations, and enough background experiences to know how to deal successfully with complex social situations. Without these skills and the maturity that comes from them, young women become especially vulnerable to acquaintance rape when they encounter the almost absolute freedom of college or independent living.

Discuss Rape Prevention Strategies With Children

There is really no absolute protection against acquaintance rape, and no way to know for certain which "nice" man will commit a rape. The best prevention techniques are awareness, assertiveness, avoidance strategies to diffuse potentially dangerous situations, and the ability to fight back, if necessary.

Parents can help prepare children by providing them with the following information about acquaintance rape prevention. See Appendix R for specific acquaintance rape prevention strategies.

Teens should understand that most acquaintance rapes begin with a non-threatening social encounter. Since most rapists are between the ages of 15 and 24 (Amir, 1977), some are likely to be in college or in young adult gathering places (such as bars or parties). College is a time when young people are beginning to explore and understand the subtleties of adult sex role interactions (British Columbia Rape Prevention Project, 1980). This is especially important since most victims and assailants come from the same neighborhood, and many rapes follow a meeting at a bar, party, or in the home of the victim or rapist (Amir, 1977).

Adolescents must be encouraged to trust their instincts. If they sense someone is potentially dangerous, they should not feel compelled to remain with him, even if he is an uncle or boyfriend. If a teen feels uncomfortable in a situation, the goal should be to get out of the situation as quickly and effectively as possible. It is better to be rude than to become a victim. Swift, decisive action early in the encounter may be the key to avoiding rape (Bart, 1981).

Women should be forthright, appropriately wary, and definite in their encounters with men. Assertive verbal

"There is really no absolute protection against acquaintance rape, and no way to know for certain which "nice" man will commit a rape."

confrontation is often helpful to avoid uncomfortable encounters (such as "Leave me alone!"). Grossman and Sutherland (1983) define assertiveness as being aware of personal rights (right to privacy, respect, not being touched against one's will) and speaking out to protect these rights.

Most women must make a conscious effort to learn assertiveness because that behavior is not a usual part of the female socialization process. A woman may view standing up for her rights as "unfeminine." Rapists often use a woman's passive behavior and fear against her. Women who are assertive, present themselves in a self assured manner, and speak up for their rights are less likely to be seen as targets of rapists (Bart, 1981).

"An important part of assertiveness includes clearly indicating what is intended with both words and actions."

An important part of assertiveness includes clearly indicating what is intended with both words and actions. If a woman says "no" with her mouth, and "yes" with her body, she is giving a mixed and inconsistent message. She must know what she wants clearly before she can ask for it.

In addition to knowing what she wants from a relationship, a woman should also know which behaviors constitute rape and in which settings acquaintance rapes are most likely to occur. Acquaintance rapes do not usually happen on the first date because the man is usually on his "best behavior" at that time. Second or third dates are more likely times for acquaintance rapes to occur because the woman has let her guard down, and the date is more likely to end in a secluded place such as one of their apartments.

The information, skills, and strategies presented here may be difficult for parents to accept. Parents are asked to give up some control over their children, teach them new and difficult concepts, and change some of their own behaviors and attitudes.

Young adults of today may experience the same types of problems at 18 that their parents faced at 25 because there are more freedoms at earlier ages in the 1980s than there were in the 1950s. It is unlikely that these 18 year olds have attained the same maturity level their parents had at 25, so they need to be prepared with more skills than their parents had to protect themselves and minimize the associated trauma.

Parents can be helpful rather than feel impotent in helping their teens cope with the difficult social situations of the 1980s and beyond. Parents must provide children with problem solving and decision making skills, and instill their values in their children. In doing this, parents may be more successful if they view their children with respect, rather than from an authoritarian perspective.

7
HOW TO ENCOURAGE SELF ESTEEM IN ADOLESCENTS

Behaviors

1. **Try to find out how the adolescent thinks others view him or her.** Effectiveness, efficiency, and ability to cope with life tasks depends on our perception of how others view us.

2. **Be "real" with the adolescent;** they will know when you don't mean what you are saying.

3. **Avoid discouragement** since this adds to a feeling of insecurity.

4. **Commend effort,** not the finished product.

5. **Encourage, rather than praise.** Praise may have an encouraging effect on some people, but it often discourages and causes anxiety and fear. Some come to depend on praise and will perform only for the recognition in ever-increasing amounts.

6. **Strive for improvement,** not perfection.

7. **Avoid chastising for failure**, because that may make an adolescent afraid to try.

8. **Mistakes should not be viewed as failures,** but rather as learning experiences.

9. **Help the adolescent come up with concrete suggestions on how to do something better** after having told them they need to improve.

10. **Stimulate and lead the adolescent,** but do not try to push him or her ahead.

11. **Understand that real adult happiness comes from self-sufficiency**.

12. **Integrate the adolescent into the group,** since we all need to feel that we are a member of some group.

13. **Do not push competition,** because if the adolescent feels that the goal is to win, but he or she loses, failure is the result.

14. **Make tasks a partnership with the adolescent rather than a mandate,** give the adolescent ownership in problem solving.

15. **Keep close track of how a task is going, intervene to improve and give praise, not just to evaluate at the completion of the task.** This way you may help to divert a problem before it becomes serious.

16. **Don't assign responsibility and significance only to those who already have responsibility**. That will reinforce the notion that a few are capable but many are incapable and it will not help develop responsibility in those with poor self esteem.

17. **Understand that discouragement is contagious.** If you are discouraged, you will transmit that feeling to those around you. Overcome your own pessimism and develop an optimistic approach to life.

18. **Smile while making eye contact with the adolescent.** This will make the adolescent feel that you are happy to be talking with him or her.

19. **Treat adolescents respectfully.** Treat them with the same respect and kindness with which you would like to be treated.

20. **Don't compare the adolescent with anyone else.**

21. **Assign tasks which are age and skill appropriate.**

22. **Build on success experiences. Build and focus on strengths,** not weaknesses.

23. **Help with problem solving,** but don't solve problems for them.

24. **Solicit the help of others, such as (peers, siblings, and family members) to help a discouraged adolescent find his or her place.**

25. **Avoid mending your own threatened ego by discouraging others or looking down on them.**

26. **Help the adolescent develop the courage to be imperfect.** We should learn from our mistakes and take them in stride, not become paralyzed by them.

27. **Don't interact with the adolescent only when he or she is doing something wrong and ignore them the rest of the time.**

28. **Separate the deed from the doer** so that a person does not equate his or her value with how well a task is completed.

Verbal Communication

1. **Say "good" or "I like what you said"** after listening to the person.

2. **Paraphrase or repeat** what the person says before making a statement of your own, this will give the adolescent the feeling that you are really listening.

3. **Refer to the person by name.**

4. **Always sandwich negative comments between two positives.** Make sure that the adolescent heard the positives by asking him or her to repeat them back to you.

(Adapted and expanded from Blum, 1984; Dreikurs, & Cassel, 1972.)

8
EMOTIONAL CONSEQUENCES OF ACQUAINTANCE RAPE

Rape is commonly perceived as an act committed by a "crazed maniac" who leaps from the bushes and violently forces himself on a defenseless victim. There is no question that this is rape, but so is forced sex between acquaintances. The misconception that one can only be raped by a stranger is not only common in our society but also among the victims of acquaintance rape.

Common Emotions Following Acquaintance Rape

Acquaintance rape victims often experience emotional trauma following the rape, but their trauma pattern frequently differs from that of stranger rape victims. There are a number of common emotional responses to rape which cause tremendous emotional and physical trauma. These include emotional shock, disbelief, embarrassment, shame, guilt, depression, powerlessness, disorientation, triggered recall, denial, fear, anxiety, and anger (Grossman and Sutherland, 1983; Hughes and Sandler, 1987).

Judith Krulewitz (1982) of Iowa State University postulates that rape victims fall into one of three emotional categories following the rape: 1) upset-anger, 2) upset-guilt, or 3) calm. Both types of "upset" victims are reported to have more long lasting problems than calm victims. They are also more likely to try to repress the incident and are less likely to accept personal responsibility for the assault than are calm victims (Krulewitz, 1982).

Barry Burkhart (1983) of Auburn University believes that acquaintance rape victims go through disorientation and repression phases. In the disorientation phase, victims experience emotional shock, manifested by a feeling of numbness or the inability to cry. Disbelief that the rape actually happened is a common feeling. The victim may feel embarrassed about what people will think. Shame associated with "feeling dirty" may lead to obsessive hand or body washing.

> *"Guilt is a very common reaction, especially among acquaintance rape victims because the victim may feel that her behavior contributed to the rape."*

Guilt is a very common reaction, especially among acquaintance rape victims because the victim may feel that her behavior contributed to the rape. Feelings of powerlessness are common among acquaintance rape victims because they feel that their judgement is questionable. All the social "cues" which helped them control their environment in the past are no longer valid. They have lost their frame of reference. Disorientation may result, making it difficult for the victim to carry out common, simple behaviors that used to be part of a daily routine. Victims may complain that they can not sit still, or that daily routines are overwhelming.

The recollection of the rape may be triggered by daily routines that remind the victim of the assailant. This is especially common among rape victims who have shared some of these routines with their assailant. A female victim may also deny or minimize the severity of the experience by trying to convince herself that "it was just a rape," and she should feel fortunate that she was not also beaten or killed.

Fear often results when the reality and consequences of the rape occur to the victim. It may be focused on many possible areas, such as pregnancy, sexually transmitted diseases, future intimacy, future mental disorientation, nightmares or recurrence of the attack because the assailant knows the victim and where to find her. Rape victims remain significantly more fearful than non-victims for long periods following the assault (Calhoun, Atkenson, and Resick, 1982).

These emotional problems often lead to anxiety which may cause physical symptoms such as difficulty in breathing, muscle tension, nightmares, ulcers, or change in eating habits. Finally, the victim may become angry enough to want to kill the assailant.

Impact of Admitting and Reporting an Acquaintance Rape

When a woman has been raped by an acquaintance, she must be able to admit that the experience was a rape in order to deal with the emotional, physical, and legal problems associated with the experience. The three stages in the process of admitting a rape are intrapersonal, interpersonal, and institutional.

The first stage, intrapersonal, involves admitting the occurrence of the rape to oneself. Many victims never do this, preferring to define the event as a bad experience. The second stage, interpersonal, is admitting the rape to someone else, such as the rape crisis center or a friend. Women tend to be more sympathetic and more willing to talk to rape victims than men (Krulweitz, 1982). This sex difference may be because males view the victim as more responsible for the rape than do females (Calhoun, Selby, and Warring, 1976). A victim may decide to stop at this stage of the reporting process, yet still seek emotional or psychological help.

The next level of admittance is institutional. This involves seeking medical attention and/or reporting the rape to the police. Victims may be able to resolve a rape without going on to this step. It may even be easier for the victim to "come to emotional terms" with the rape if she does not have to face the "second assault" by the legal system to try to get a conviction. Some law enforcement officials feel that the trial is more traumatic for the victim than the actual rape. Some women choose to only report the event to the police, but not seek prosecution or a conviction. Some victims take long periods of time to report the event to the police, but may seek medical help almost immediately.

If a victim of an acquaintance rape does not confront the emotional trauma that she is encountering, she is likely to continue to have emotional problems in the future. In fact, acquaintance rape victims tend to have many more psychological disturbances such as greater depression, guilt, and a higher incidence of sexual dysfunction than other women (Burkhart, 1983). Many victims become either sex avoidant or less discriminating in their choice of sexual partners, explaining that their sexual contacts do not matter any more. This reflects a feeling that she is not in control of her life, and that she is not a valuable enough person to have the right of choice in sexual behavior.

The most powerful determinant in deciding whether to report the experience as a rape seems to be the degree of force used. Having no prior acquaintance with the assailant also is associated with greater willingness to report the rape to the police (Skelton, and Burkhart, 1980). Since most acquaintance rapes occur without associated violence and the victim knows the assailant, the report rate or interpersonal disclosure rate is much lower for acquaintance rapes than for stranger rapes. Burkhart (1983) estimates that only one in 100 acquaintance rapes is reported.

There are four reasons victims do not identify acquaintance rape as such: concern for the rapist, the victim assumes some of the responsibility, the social stereotype of rape, and the victim tries to protect herself from the mental anguish associated with being classified as a rape victim.

Concern for the rapist and his family may prevent a victim from reporting to the police. The assailant would probably encounter negative publicity which could damage his reputation

(Amir, 1971). In addition, if the rapist denies the rape, mutual friends of the victim and rapist will be forced to believe one or the other; the victim may lose a large part of her support system if she is not believed. If the victim reports the rape to the police and presses charges, she may fear retribution from the rapist if he is acquitted or following his release from incarceration.

Some victims may feel they contributed to the rape in a number of ways. Common examples include: inviting the rapist home for something other than sex, agreeing to go out with him, dressing in a certain way, or even having had sex with him in the past. It is sometimes difficult for an acquaintance rape victim to believe that rape occurs any time she is forced to have intercourse against her will (with the exclusion of wives and past lovers in some states that do not consider these events as legal rapes).

When force is used, however, women feel less responsible for the sexual outcome because they were forced to comply with their assailant's physical demands (Skelton & Burkhart, 1980). The social stereotype of rape developed from the notion that women are responsible for the outcome of sexual interactions unless their responsibility has been usurped (Weis & Borges, 1975; Klemmack & Klemmack, 1976). Because violence is often not a part of acquaintance rapes, this stereotype may not apply. The greater the degree of force used in an acquaintance rape, the less embarrassed the victim is about the experience. The more liberal the victim's attitude toward women is, the more likely she is to report a rape. If a woman chooses not to report the event to the police, she faces greater skepticism by the law, medical professionals, and her friends (Bohmer, 1973; Schwendinger & Schwendinger, 1974; Field, 1978).

A victim may not define what has happened to her as rape to protect herself from the emotional aftermath of rape. The emotional phases through which victims pass following a rape are traumatic. If she is able to assume any responsibility for the event, she will not define the experience as rape and may be able to avoid rape's emotional aftermath.

When a woman mistrusts her judgement following an acquaintance rape, she may start questioning her selection of friends and acquaintances and doubt her ability to judge the motives of others. Problems arise as victims find it difficult to have to question every decision they make as being possibly inappropriate.

The Contribution of Socialization

Men are rewarded for being persistent sexually, and women are accustomed to having their refusal challenged. College men generally indicate that a woman must refuse sex (say "no") more than once for them to stop "pushing." The number of refusals depends on the force with which she says "no," the consistency of her verbal and non-verbal messages, and the couple's past socialization.

"Men are rewarded for being persistent sexually, and women are accustomed to having their refusal challenged."

Some women feel that they have contributed to the confusion about their desires by providing inconsistent messages. It is difficult for a woman to give a clear and consistent message about sex if she is not really sure of what she wants. The messages she gets from different sectors of society may be inconsistent. Women tend to assume some of the blame for undesired intercourse, in which case they will not call it "rape" even if all of the legal elements for a rape are present.

Most women find it hard to think of themselves as rape victims, especially because there are many emotional problems and serious difficulties associated with having been raped. Lack of information about the definition of legal rape also contributes to women not realizing their experience was rape.

The problems which contribute to and result from defining rape as simply a bad experience will not be eliminated until both men and women are educated about the legal definition of rape, rights of individuals, value of women, assertiveness, clear communication, and the understanding of the non-verbal messages of others. Our society risks "losing" much and "gaining" little if this pattern continues. Both men and women suffer from the victimization and degradation of women. Any man who has a wife, daughter, sister, mother, or female friend may be touched by this issue. Men can also be victims or unwitting assailants of acquaintance rapes. The collective mental health of society will benefit from the results of valuing women as equals and educating all members about the rights of people.

9
RECOMMENDATIONS FOR COLLEGE POLICIES AND PROCEDURES

There are several ways college and university administrations view and respond to acquaintance rape and sexual assault. Many do not acknowledge that acquaintance rape exists on their campus or that there is even such a thing as acquaintance rape. Some view it as a problem, but are not sure how to deal with it, particularly when both parties agree that they had sexual intercourse but do not agree on mutual consent. Still other universities treat acquaintance rape as any other crime: that it will not be tolerated and the offender will be expelled from campus.

Each of these approaches to acquaintance rape is accompanied by implicit messages which reflect the administrations' attitude toward acceptable male and female behavior. How administrations deal with acquaintance rape cases that are brought to their attention will determine the extent to which future cases will be reported.

A recent example at Syracuse University illustrates these points. In 1986 a junior football player was legally charged with two counts of first degree rape and one count of first degree sodomy against a first year female student. The district attorney refused to present the case to the grand jury. The athlete then pled guilty to sexual misconduct. The judge sentenced him to three years probation and three hundred hours of community service. An administrative tribunal from Syracuse University advised no sanctions; he could continue to attend the University, play football, and retain his scholarship. The University Chancellor overruled this decision and prohibited him from playing his first five games.

Some men on that campus may have received the message from these actions that you may do what you like to women, even if it is against the law. Some may have thought that this applies only if you are an athlete or on scholarship. Syracuse women received the message that the University will not take them seriously if they come forward to report sexual assault or rape by an acquaintance. If Syracuse had dealt harshly with the athlete, the message would have been different; that women are believable, that sex is not something men have a right to regardless of the woman's wishes, and that men will be held accountable for their actions.

Many university administrators are concerned about taking a "hard line" stand in these cases, even if the law has been broken, perhaps because they believe that the man who broke the law did not know that what he was doing was wrong. Societal messages have provided some men with the notions that men must always be ready and willing to have sex, that a woman never means "no," and that sex is their right if they spend a great deal of money on their dates. Some men also feel that a woman is asking for sex if she gets drunk, goes back to a man's apartment, or asks him back to hers. New York Law is clear that rape is forced sexual intercourse with a woman against her will and without her consent, or when a woman is fearful for her safety or her life (Penal Law of New York State, 1988). She does not have to say "no" more than once, and she does not have to explain why she was in the situation in which the rape occurred.

Rapes are divided into two categories by law: simple and aggravated (Estrich, 1987). Simple rape involves no force or violence, a single assailant, and no other crimes are committed at the same time, such as murder or assault. Aggravated rape is a situation in which a woman is threatened, attacked by more than one man, a victim of force or violence, and/or another crime is committed at the time. Of the two types, simple rapes are very rarely reported to the police, and rarely result in conviction (Estrich, 1987). If they do result in conviction, the verdict is often overturned on appeal (Rowland, 1985).

This distinction is in part responsible for the very low report rate of sexual abuse to the legal system.

However, several studies of college campuses nationwide have reported that approximately 20% of college women will be victims of sexual abuse at some point during their college career (Koss, 1987; Burkhart, 1983; Parrot, 1985). Burkhart (1983) also estimates that fewer than one in 100 acquaintance rapes are actually reported to the authorities. Some women do not report because they believe that the legal system will not do anything to the rapist and may, in fact, blame the victim. Others do not talk about the crime because they fear they will not be believed.

"Many people do not believe that an event was rape if the woman is not bruised, not hysterical, and the offender was not a stranger (Johnson, 1985)."

Many people do not believe that an event was rape if the woman is not bruised, not hysterical, and the offender was not a stranger (Johnson, 1985). However, these factors are not necessary for a rape to have occurred. College administrators may know this intellectually, but they find it hard to treat acquaintance rape as a crime. There are several reasons for this.

First, in this day of declining numbers of applicants, they may be worried that negative publicity about the rape will hurt their enrollment figures. Second, they may not have a policy on sexual conduct on campus, and may not even be sure what the law says regarding this issue. Third, they may be worried about being sued by the man if the university deals harshly with him, but the court finds him not guilty. Finally, they may be worried about wrongly accusing someone of rape, and "ruining his life."

Administrators may also be in conflict with the notion of acquaintance rape from a personal perspective. They may have been in a situation where a woman said "no" but meant "yes," and they are generalizing their experience to others. They may also have forced women to have sex against their protests, and do not think of themselves as rapists, and thus cannot define this as rape.

The following recommendations should address these institutional concerns while protecting all students, both male and female.

1. Develop a university policy regarding acceptable sexual behavior, similar to those for alcohol and drugs. The policy should clearly outline penalties which will follow specific behaviors.

2. Make the policy known to all students during new student orientation in an oral and written presentation.

3. Provide alcohol free events for student participation. Discourage alcohol use.

4. Provide programs for all students on acquaintance rape and prevention strategies early in their college careers. Also provide follow up programs.

5. Present these programs to men as well as women. Rape will not stop until men stop raping. Telling women how to avoid rape will not stop it.

6. The first violation of the policy should be dealt with swiftly and harshly, even if the case does not result in a criminal conviction.

7. Provide the woman with as much support as she needs, but do not pressure her to pursue a course of action with which she is uncomfortable. If she wants to press charges, help her with that process but respect her wishes if she does not want to pursue legal recourse.

8. Establish a position on campus for someone to train safety officers and counselors, confer with university counsel, monitor these cases, and support those involved.

9. Reevaluate the role and structure of the fraternity system.

10. Appoint a coordinator of sexual assault prevention services on campus.

11. Conduct research on your campus to determine the extent of the problem.

These procedures will not eliminate the problem of acquaintance rape on campus. Interim procedures may also be necessary to deal with offenders before all students have been exposed to information on acquaintance rape presented at new student orientation. More women will probably come forward as victims, not to press charges, but to utilize the counseling services available to them. Eventually less men will consider it acceptable to take advantage of women sexually, thus making universities a better place for students to study, learn, and develop into well rounded adults.

Although most institutions which have expressed a concern over this issue do not have policies, those which do often have incomplete policies, or have them hidden in a section dealing with other behaviors (such as sexual harassment). Sexual abuse does not fit well in the sexual harassment section of university policy because sexual harassment usually covers situations dealing with employment or professor-student relationships, while most sexual abuse takes place between students. If the policy is under a section other than sexual abuse, it is not easy to find within the table of contents or the index of the policy manual. Therefore, if a student wants to know what the policy is, he or she will have a difficult time locating the section which relates to sexual abuse.

Most established policies do not indicate sanctions which are likely to be applied. Policies should refer to the legal statutes of the state where the institution is located and must define terms such as sexual abuse, acquaintance rape, and consent so a student reading the policy clearly understands which behaviors violate the policy.

For example, the policy may state that "Forcing a person to have sex without consent is considered sexual abuse." A reader may assume that if a woman gets drunk and passes out then sex in that case is not sexual abuse because she did not resist or say no. Yet, the law views being passed out as a situation in which a woman can not give consent, and therefore, is sexual abuse.

"Acquaintance rape or sexual abuse cases rarely go to trial because the police or the district attorney do not believe there is sufficient evidence."

Acquaintance rape or sexual abuse cases rarely go to trial because the police or the district attorney do not believe there is sufficient evidence. Of those which do go to trial, very few result in convictions. It is not unusual for such convictions to be overturned on appeal. With such poor odds of ever reaching justice, it is not surprising that very few women ever report acquaintance sexual abuse to the police.

These trends are true of all "simple" rapes (those with no violence, single attacker, and no other crime committed at the time). The report and conviction rates are much higher for aggravated rape cases, but these are not as likely to occur on college campuses.

One of the reasons that report rates are so low for acquaintance rapes is that both men and women may think that if a woman has been drinking and passes out, she "is asking for it." Victims are also blamed for acquaintance rapes for inviting the man back to her apartment, or agreeing to go back to his, or previous consensual sex with him. Many women do not know the law, and therefore believe what others have told them about the woman being to blame.

It is impossible to tell the extent of acquaintance sexual abuse on a campus without research at that institution.

There is not a strong correlation between having a campus policy on acquaintance rape and high report rates versus no policy and low report rates. Several factors may account for this.

Even if a policy exists, it may not be well publicized, and students may be unaware of it. If the policy is known to students but is not carried out in the event of a violation, victims may be less likely to report a case of sexual abuse. If there is a policy and harsh sanctions are carried out, there may be a reduction in the rate of acquaintance sexual abuse, but few schools have taken the necessary steps to achieve this reduction now.

Most victims of acquaintance sexual assault do not want to have the assailant end up in jail, but they would like some retribution to prevent him from committing acquaintance rape with others. Many victims are primarily interested in getting emotional help so that they can continue with their lives and put the assault behind them emotionally. They believe that going to the police will add to their emotional trauma, rather than reduce it. Instead they may choose to talk to someone at the counseling center or a sympathetic friend, if they talk to anyone at all.

In 1987 the author surveyed 99 institutions to determine the incidence of acquaintance rape policies at college campuses. The institutions surveyed were not representative of all colleges and universities in the nation and the respondents primarily represented those with an interest in working toward the elimination of this problem. Even though all 99 institutions that were surveyed expressed concern about this problem, the response rate was less than 40%. This may be because many institutions are uncomfortable discussing their programs and policies (or lack thereof). The respondents probably have done more work toward the elimination of acquaintance sexual abuse on campuses than the rest of the colleges and universities in the nation because of their expressed interest in acquaintance rape prevention.

Conclusion

Acquaintance sexual abuse on college campuses is quite common, although it is rarely reported to the campus police. Many institutions, therefore, do not think that they have a problem on their campus. As a result, many do not have official policies against such behaviors. Students are usually aware that acquaintance sexual abuse is tolerated on campuses, and that the

*"Acquaintance
sexual abuse
cases will not
stop until
institutions of
higher education
take this problem
seriously."*

legal system will usually not help the victim obtain a conviction in a criminal court.

Acquaintance sexual abuse cases will not stop until institutions of higher education take this problem seriously. The first step toward the elimination of this problem is the development of a campus policy on sexual abuse, with related sanctions made clear to students. In addition, colleges and universities must determine the extent of the problem on their campus through research. Educational efforts must be made to inform men and women about acceptable forms of sexual interaction. Finally, when a case is reported, the victim must receive support, and if the allegations are proven, the assailant should be dealt with to the fullest extent the campus policy permits. This will give the message to others who would commit a similar act that such behavior is not acceptable on that college campus.

ASSEMBLY CONCURRENT RESOLUTION NO. 46

RESOLUTION CHAPTER 105

Assembly Concurrent Resolution No. 46—Relative to rape on university or college campuses.

[Filed with Secretary of State September 14, 1987.]

LEGISLATIVE COUNSEL'S DIGEST

ACR 46, Hayden. Rapes on college or university campuses.

This measure would request all institutions of higher education to take specified action with respect to assisting rape victims and publicizing rapes that occur on their college or university campuses.

WHEREAS, A 1985 national survey of over 6,000 students on 32 college campuses revealed that one in eight women have been raped; and

WHEREAS, That study indicated that 85 percent of these incidents occurred among students who knew one another and 5 percent of the attacks involved more than one assailant; and

WHEREAS, Three-quarters of the victims of acquaintance rape did not identify their experience as rape and none of the males involved believed they had committed a crime; and

WHEREAS, Forty-five percent of the males who committed acquaintance rape said they would repeat the experience; and

WHEREAS, More than one-third of the women raped did not discuss the experience with anyone and more than 90 percent of them did not report the incident to the police; and

WHEREAS, Another national study of campus gang rapes shows that in most instances, the men involved received little or no punishment, and

WHEREAS, Most academic institutions in California do not have formal policies or procedures that deal adequately with acquaintance rape or gang rape; and

WHEREAS, Academic institutions have a legal and moral responsibility to protect the safety of members of their academic communities; now, therefore, be it

Resolved by the Assembly of the State of California, the Senate thereof concurring, That all institutions of higher education in the state should provide information to victims of alleged incidents of rape regarding available options that he or she may pursue, and that the institution of higher education should respond promptly to the option selected by the victim; and be it further

Resolved, That all institutions of higher education in the state should establish and utilize clear and consistent sexual assault policies which may be incorporated into the current disciplinary policies of each campus that do both of the following:

Res. Ch. 105

(a) Provide an institutional disciplinary process based on the principle of due process, which shall include a disciplinary hearing.

(b) Set forth and respect the rights of victims, such as the following:

(1) Equal rights, with the accused, in determining whether the hearing shall be open or closed. When there is disagreement, the hearing officer shall determine whether the hearing shall be open or closed in a manner consistent with the due process rights of the accused.

(2) The ability to have a person of the victim's choice accompany the victim throughout the disciplinary hearing.

(3) The right to be present during the entire hearing.

(4) The right not to have his or her past sexual history introduced as part of the testimony, except that the past sexual history of the victim shall be permitted if offered as evidence of the character or trait of character of the victim for the purposes described in Section 1103 of the Evidence Code.

(5) The right to a prompt relocation of one of the parties, in a manner consistent with the terms of the university facility contract or dormitory contract when the accused and the victim live in the same university facility or dormitory; and be it further

Resolved, That all institutions of higher education should develop, publicize, and enforce clear and consistent policies for taking appropriate actions against members of the campus community who participate, directly or indirectly, in rape that occurs on the property of the institution or at a campus-related function or activity. The penalties should include, but need not be limited to, suspension or expulsion for persons found, by the academic institution or a judicial court, to have committed the crime of rape and speedy removal of alleged assailants who live in the same dormitory or other campus housing as a victim; and be it further

Resolved, That all institutions of higher education should add specific language to the student codes of conduct and the dormitory rules and regulations prohibiting rape and other forms of sexual battery and specifying the penalties for the commission of these crimes; and be it further

Resolved, That all institutions of higher education should provide all freshman students and dormitory, fraternity, and sorority residents with information or annual seminars that include, but are not limited to, the following:

(1) The legal definition of rape.

(2) Student, acquaintance, and gang rape statistics.

(3) Penalties for rape; and be it further

Resolved, That all institutions of higher education in California with counseling centers that receive financial support from the institution should maintain at least one staff member who has competency in the most current therapeutic approach to acquaintance rape. This counseling should be offered in a timely manner; and be it further

Res. Ch. 105

Resolved, That all institutions of higher education in California with counseling centers on campus and in the community should develop a comprehensive data collection system to provide campus and community members with information on the incidents of sexual assault. To the extent data is available, it shall include, but not be limited to, all of the following information:

(a) The number of student rape victims coming to the center.

(b) Whether the assailant was a stranger or an acquaintance.

(c) Whether the rape was a gang rape.

(d) Whether the crime occurred on campus or at a campus-related event. Every campus should publicize the results and should report the results to its respective systemwide office or its statewide membership association. Those systemwide offices and membership associations should make a comprehensive report available to the Legislature; and be it further

Resolved, That "rape" for the purposes of this resolution means rape as defined in Section 261 of the Penal Code and that "acquaintance rape" for the purposes of this resolution means rape as defined in Section 261 of the Penal Code that is committed by an assailant who is known to the victim; and be it further

Resolved, That the Chief Clerk of the Assembly transmit copies of this resolution to each institution of higher education in this state.

STATE OF NEW YORK
SENATE - ASSEMBLY

S. 8772   A. 11755

SENATE — ASSEMBLY

May 21, 1990

IN SENATE -- Introduced by Sens. LAVALLE, N. LEVY -- read twice and ordered printed, and when printed to be committed to the Committee on Rules

IN ASSEMBLY -- Introduced by COMMITTEE ON RULES -- (at request of M. of A. E. C. Sullivan, Weinstein) -- read once and referred to the Committee on Higher Education

AN ACT to amend the education law, in relation to sexual assault prevention and campus security

The People of the State of New York, represented in Senate and Assembly, do enact as follows:

1   Section 1. Subdivision 1-a of section 6450 of the education law, as
2   added by a chapter of the laws of 1990, amending the education law
3   relating to advisory committees on campus security, as proposed in
4   legislative bill numbers S. 7170 -- A. 9624, is amended to read as
5   follows:
6   1-a. Sexual assault prevention information. (a) The [governing board
7   of each college shall provide information to incoming students about]
8   trustees or governing board of each college shall inform incoming stu-
9   dents about sexual assault prevention measures through programs which
10 may include workshops, seminars, discussion groups, and film presenta-
11 tions, in order to disseminate information about sexual assault, promote
12 discussion, encourage reporting of incidents of sexual assault, and
13 facilitate prevention of such incidents. Such information shall include,
14 but not be limited to: (1) the applicable laws, ordinances and regula-
15 tions on sex offenses, (2) the penalties for commission of sex offenses,
16 (3) the procedures in effect at the college for dealing with sex of-
17 fenses, (4) the availability of counseling and other support services
18 for the victims of sex offenses, (5) the nature of and common circum-
19 stances relating to sex offenses on college campuses, and (6) the
20 methods the college employs to advise and to update students about
21 security procedures.

EXPLANATION--Matter in *italics* (underscored) is new; matter in brackets
[ ] is old law to be omitted.

LBD03958-12-0

S. 8772   A. 11755

1   (b) Pursuant to the requirements set forth in paragraph (a) of this
2 subdivision, each college shall file a report annually on its compliance
3 with this subdivision with the commissioner.
4   § 2. Paragraphs (b) and (c) of subdivision 4 of section 6450 of the
5 education law, as added by a chapter of the laws of 1990, amending the
6 education law relating to advisory committees on campus security, as
7 proposed in legislative bill numbers S. 7170 -- A. 9624, is amended to
8 read as follows:
9   (b) Such committee shall consist of a minimum of six members, at least
10 half of whom shall be female[,] ⅃ one-third of [whom] the committee
11 shall be appointed from a list of students that contains at least twice
12 the number to be appointed which is provided by the largest student gov-
13 ernance organization on such campus, one-third [of whom] thereof shall
14 be appointed from a list of faculty members that contains twice the num-
15 ber to be appointed which is provided by the largest faculty organiza-
16 tion on such campus, and one-third of whom shall be selected by the pre-
17 sident or chief administrative officer.
18   (c) The committee shall review current campus security policies and
19 procedures and make recommendations for their improvement. It shall spe-
20 cifically review current policies and procedures (1) for educating the
21 campus community, including security personnel and those persons who ad-
22 vise or supervise students, about sexual assault pursuant to subdivision
23 one-a of this section, (2) for educating the campus community about per-
24 sonal safety and crime prevention, (3) for reporting sexual assaults and
25 dealing with victims during investigations, (4) for referring com-
26 plaints to appropriate authorities, (5) for counseling victims, and (6)
27 for responding to inquiries from concerned persons.
28   § 3. This act shall take effect on the same date as such chapter of
29 the laws of 1990 takes effect.

MEMORANDUM IN SUPPORT OF LEGISLATION
Submitted in accordance with Assembly Rule III, Section 1(e)

Bill Number: Assembly   Senate
                                 Memo on original draft of bill x
                                 Memo on amended bill

Sponsors: Members of Assembly   E.C. Sullivan
          Senators: LaValle

Introduced at the request of:

TITLE OF BILL:

AN ACT to amend the education law, in relation to sexual assault
prevention and campus security.

PURPOSE OF GENERAL IDEA OF BILL:

To clarify the intent of S. 7170/A. 9624 which requires colleges to
inform incoming students about sexual assault prevention and to
establish advisory committees on campus security.

SUMMARY OF SPECIFIC PROVISIONS:

This legislation amends S. 7170/A. 9624 to state that the trustees or
governing board of each college shall inform incoming students about
sexual assault prevention measures through programs which may include
workshops, seminars, discussion groups, and film presentations, in
order to disseminate information about sexual assault, promote
discussion, encourage reporting of incidents, and facilitate prevention
of sexual assault.

The advisory committee on campus security shall review current policies
and procedures for educating the campus community, including security
personnel and persons who advise or supervise students about, sexual
assault prevention.

JUSTIFICATION:

This legislation clarifies that the intent of S.7170/ A. 9624 is for
colleges and universities of this State to offer programs aimed at the
prevention of sexual assault among their college students and not
simply to provide pamphlets to incoming students.   The problem of
sexual assault on college campuses is extremely serious and cannot be
ignored by college officials.   Educating students is an effective
method for preventing tragic occurrences of sexual assault.

The second amendment proposed to this bill would expand the scope of
the review by the campus advisory committee to include a review of
current policies and procedures for educating the campus community
including security personnel and those persons who advise or supervise
students about the institution's sexual assault policies.

PRIOR LEGISLATIVE HISTORY:

New bill.

FISCAL IMPLICATIONS:

None.

EFFECTIVE DATE:

The same date as such Chapter of the Laws of 1990.

10
SUMMARY OF RECOMMENDATIONS

I.   Administrative Policies and Procedures

   A.   Administrative Response

      1.   Administration must take a tough stand with assailants.
      2.   Eliminate organizations which commit or support gang or acquaintance rapes.
      3.   Carefully examine the fraternity system and structure, and revise if necessary.
      4.   The first violation of the policy should be dealt with swiftly and harshly. Even if the case does not result in a criminal conviction, if the assailant violated the university code of conduct, the university policy should be carried out.
      5.   Establish a position on campus for someone to train safety officers and counselors, confer with university counsel, monitor these cases, and support those involved in those cases.

6. Create a rapid response team to be mobilized in the event of a reported rape.
7. Provide proactive and preventive media coverage rather than reactive media coverage.

B. Personnel Recommendations

1. Coordination with local police agencies.
2. Some mechanism to collect and disseminate accurate statistics.
3. Implementation of security measures to reduce the likelihood of acquaintance sexual assault victimization.
4. Organizations in a Task Force or Coalition.
    a. Dean of Student's Office
    b. Residence Life
    c. Public Safety
    d. Health Center
        – Health Education Department
        – Psychological Services
        – Sex Counselor
        – Medical Personnel
    e. Academic Faculty
        – Women's Studies
        – Psychology
        – Sociology
        – Human Development and Family Studies
        – Nursing
        – Political Science
        – Philosophy
        – Criminal Justice
        – Law
        – Social Work
        – Human Service Studies
        – Medicine
        – Physical Education
        – Health Education
    f. Local Rape Crisis Center
    g. Religious Organizations on Campus
    h. Office of Equal Opportunity
    i. Students

C. Personal Safety Recommendations

   1. Public Safety
      a. "Blue light" direct phones to Public Safety throughout campus.
      b. Special free busses after dark with stops at "blue lights"
      c. "Safe Houses" (green light program)
      d. Escort service at night
      e. Training for safety officers

D. Financial

   1. Allocate funds to the prevention of the problem.
   2. Support research to determine the extent of the problem on your campus.

E. Policy

   1. Develop a university regarding acceptable sexual behavior, similar to those for alcohol and drugs. The policy should clearly outline penalties which will follow specific behaviors.
   2. Establish a written protocol for dealing with sexual assault cases, including:
      a. college policy regarding sexual assault on campus
      b. notification procedures and designated personnel to be notified (with victim consent)
      c. legal reporting requirements and procedures
      d. services available for victims
      e. on and off campus resources available
      f. procedures for ongoing case management
      g. procedures for guaranteeing confidentiality
   3. Return to in loco parentis policies which were common 20 years ago intended to protect students
   4. Judicial Board recommendations
      a. Visitors to campus should be covered under the policy
      b. Sanctions may be applied against organizations which condone rape or sexual assault

       c.   Judicial board members should be trained regarding sexual assault law and definitions of terms

       d.   Terms such as "lack of consent," "rape," and "sexual assault" be defined in the campus code of conduct

5. Hearing Recommendations
   a. Closed hearing
   b. Victim permitted to be present during the hearing
   c. Victim permitted to have counsel or advisor available during the hearing
   d. Rape shield laws should apply
   e. Witnesses should be made know to both sides 72 hours before the hearing
   f. Allow the victim's testimony to be videotaped
   g. Develop a written agreement with the DA that a campus hearing will not violate the defendant's 5th amendment rights

6. Treatment of the accused
   a. Minimum Sentences
   b. Prohibiting graduation while charges are pending against the accused
   c. Preventing registration for future semesters until the condition of the sentence has been satisfied
   d. The accused may be moved from his residence hall at the discretion of the victim

F. Services for Victims

1. Provide the victim (usually a woman) with as much support as she needs, but do not pressure her to pursue a course of actin with which she is uncomfortable.
2. Establish a comprehensive program for assisting victims.
3. Referral to free therapists, trained in acquaintance rape.
4. Availability of a trained victim advocate.
5. Counseling

       a.   Counseling for acquaintance rape victims

       b.   Acquaintance rape victim support groups

       c.   Support groups for significant others of rape victims

       d.   Victim's Assistance Advocates

6. Have trained medical personnel available to provide care for the victim and to collect evidence if necessary.

II. Educational Efforts

A. Training for faculty and staff

1. Train support staff (residence life, counselors, OEO officers, public safety, etc.) to deal with this problem.
2. Train medical personnel to examine and provide services to acquaintance rape victims.
3. Encourage faculty to discuss this issue in their classes.

B. Provide programs for all students on acquaintance rape and strategies

1. Discuss acquaintance rape in orientation programs for new students
2. Provide programs in single sex living units, such as residence halls, fraternities, and sororities.
3. Make women's self defense classes available
4. Offer assertiveness training for males and females
5. Provide self-esteem programs for males and females
6. Offer programs on the dysfunction of sex role stereotyping
7. Develop programs for all male groups which perpetuate this type of behavior.
8. Hold a special orientation session each semester with international students to describe appropriate behavior toward women on campus
9. Make the policy known to all students during new student orientation in an oral and written presentation.

C. Programs should reflect administration philosophy regarding acquaintance rape issues.

 1. Address these programs to men as well as women. Rape will not stop until men stop raping. Telling women how to avoid rape will not stop it.
 2. Inform students that they may be civilly as well as legally liable for psychological as well as physical injuries resulting from harassment or acquaintance rape.
 3. Involve fraternities and sororities in the planning and implementation of programs.
 4. Involve the student government in funding, sponsorship, and/or implementation of rape education programs.
 5. Appeal directly to male campus leaders, fraternity presidents, sports team captains to get involved, they may be able to influence others.
 6. Ensure that there is a mechanism to coordinate all these prevention efforts.

D. Written materials should be developed and disseminated

 1. Develop and provide an informal brochure for all students explaining what victims should do.
 2. Admissions literature should address the problem, and state that the campus administration is committed to preventing and prosecuting acquaintance rape.

E. Information should be delivered in a variety of traditional and nontraditional ways.

 1. Utilize alternative information and delivery programs
    a. Printed Media
    b. Computer Accessible Information
    c. Nonprinted media
 2. Create a speakers bureau of interested faculty, students, and staff, and train them appropriately. Provide presenters with a stipend.

3. Organize a campus wide speak out to sensitize the campus community
4. Offer a program of a "mock trial" of an acquaintance rape.
5. Have representatives from the local women's center provide programs or assistance in planning programs.
6. Post announcements of programs in males living quarters, locker rooms, etc.
7. Males should co-facilitate programs on acquaintance rape.
8. Develop a master list of all resources and programs available relating to acquaintance rape programs for the use of counselors, health professionals, students, and researchers.
9. Publicize incidence data regarding acquaintance rapes and penalties in the campus news paper.
10. Use campus radio and TV to make public service announcements.

F. Alcohol Related Efforts

1. Provide nonalcoholic events for students
2. Discourage the consumption of alcohol by students

11
REFERENCES

Adams, C.; Fay, J.; and Loren-Martin, J. (1984, Fall). "It's Rape Even if You Know the Guy." *Family Life Educator*, 3, (1), 4-7.

Amir, M. (1981). *Patterns in Forcible Rape*. Chicago: University of Chicago Press.

Antaki, C., and Brewin, C. (eds.) (1982). *Attributions and Psychological Change*. London: Academic Press.

Bancroft, K.; Benson, J.; Brown, A.; Edwards, S.; Foster, L.; and Plamer, L. (1982, September). *Working Against Rape*. (updated and revised by L. Harper).

Barrett, K. (1982, September). "Date Rape." *MS.*, 48-51, 130.

Bart, P. (1981). "A Study of Women Who Both Were Raped and Avoided Rape." *Journal of Social Issues*. 37, (4), 123-137.

Bateman, P. (1982). *Acquaintance Rape: Awareness and Prevention*. Seattle: Alternatives to Fear.

Beherns, D., (1981, April). *Glamour*. 248-249, 315, 317-318.

Beneke, T. (1982). *Men On Rape*. New York: St. Martins Press.

Blum, G. (1984). "Feeling Good About Yourself, Myths and Realities of Self Esteem." *Impact '83-84*.

Bohmer, C. (1973). "Judicial Attitudes Toward Rape Victims." *Judicature*, 57, 303-307.

Bowden, M. (1983, September 11). "The Incident at Alpha Ta Omega." *The Philadelphia Inquirer*.

British Columbia Police Commission (1980). *Rape Prevention Resource Manual*. British Columbia Rape Prevention Project, Rape Relief. MTI Teleprograms.

Burkhart, B. (1983, December). *Acquaintance Rape Statistics and Prevention*. A paper presented at the Acquaintance Rape and Prevention on Campus Conference in Louisville, Kentucky.

Calhoun, L.G.; Selby, J.W.; and Warring, L.J. (1976). "Social Perception of the Victims Causal Role in Rape: An Exemploratory Examination of Four Factors." *Human Relations*, 29, (6), 517-526.

Calhoun, K.S.; Atkenson, B.M.; and Resick, P.A. (1982). "A Longitudinal Examination of Fear Reactions in Victims of Rape." *Journal of Counseling Psychology*, 29, (6); 655-61.

Crandall, V.C., and Crandall, B.W. (1983). "Maternal and Childhool behaviors as antecedents of Internal-External Control Perceptions in Young Adulthood in Research With the Locus of Control Construct," Volume 2, *Developments and Social Problems*. Academic Press.

Dreikurs, R., and Cassel, P. (1972). *Discipline Without Tears*, Chapter 6.

Ehrhart, J. and Sandler, B. (1984). *Campus Gang Rape: Party Games?* Washington, D.C.: U.S. Government Printing Office.

Elkind, D. (1967). "Egocentrism in Adolescence." *Child Development*, 38, 1025-1034.

Erikson, E.H. (1968). *Identity, Youth, and Crisis*. New York: W.W. Norton.

Estrich, S. (1987). *Real Rape*. Cambridge: Harvard University Press.

FBI. (1984). *Uniform Crime Reports*. Washington, D.C.: U.S. Government Printing Office.

Feild, H.S. (1978). "Attitudes toward rape: A comparative analysis of police, rapist, crisis counselors, and citizens." *Journal of Personality and Social Psychology*, 36, 156-179.

Friedenberg, E.Z. (1959). *The Vanishing Adolescent*. Boston: Beacon Press.

Gecas, V. (1972). "Parental Behavior and Contextual Variations in Adolescent Self Esteem." *Sociometry*, 35, 332-345.

Giarrusso, R.; Johnson, P.; Goodchilds, J.; and Zellman, G. (1979). *Adolescent Cues and Signals: Sexual Assault*. Paper presented to a symposium of the Wester Psychological Association Meeting, San Diego, CA.

Grossman, R., and Sutherland, J. (eds.) (1983). *Surviving Sexual Assault*. New York: Congdon & Weed, Inc.

Grossman, A.N., and Birnbaum, H.J. (1983). Surviving Sexual Assault. New York: Congdon and Weed, Inc.

Groth, A.N., and Birnbaum, H.J. (1979). *Men Who Rape: Psychology of the Offender, Patterns of Rape*. Prenum.

Herzberger, S.D.; Dix, T., Erlebacher, A.; and Ginsberg, M. (1981). "A Developmental Study of Social Self-Conceptions in Adolescence: Impressions and Misimpressions." *Merrill-Palmer Quarterly*, 27,(1), 15-29.

Hite, S. (1976). *The Hite Report: A Nationwide Study of Female Sexuality*. New York: Dell.

Hite, S. (1981). *The Hite Report on Male Sexuality.* New York: Knopf.

Hughes, J.O., and Sandler, B.R. (1987). *"Friends" Raping Friends: It could Happen to You.* Washington, D.C.: Association of American Colleges, Project on the Status and Education of Women.

Johnson, K.M. (1985). *If You Are Raped.* Holmes Beach, Florida: Learning Publications.

Katz, S. Mazur, M. (1979). *Understanding the Rape Victim: A Synthesis of Findings.* New York: John Wiley.

Klemmack, S.H. and Klemmack, D.L. (1976). "The Social Definition of Rape." In J.J. Walker and S.L. Bradsky (Eds.), *Sexual Assault.* Lexington, MA: D.C. Heath.

Koss, M.P., Gidycz, C.A., and Wisinewski, N. (1987). "The Scope of Rape: Incidence and Prevalence of Sexual Aggression and Victimization in a National Sample of Higher Education Students." *Journal of Consulting and Clinical Psychology,* 55(2), 162-170.

Koss, M., and Oros, C. (1982). "Sexual Experience Survey: A Research Instrument Invenstigating Sexual Aggression and Victimization." *Journal of Counseling Psychology,* 50(3), 455-457.

Koss, M. and Harvey. (1987). *The Rape Victim.* New York: Viking Press.

Krulewitz, J.E. (1982). "Reactions to Rape Victims: Effects of Rape Cricumstances, Victim's Emotional Response, and Sex of Helper." *Journal of Counseling Psychology,* 29, (6); 645-54.

Lefcourt, H.M. (1976). *Locus of Control - Current Trends in Theory and Research.* New York: John Wiley & Sons.

Lewin, K. (1936). *A Dynamic Theory of Personality*. New York: McGraw Hill.

Louden, D.M. (1977). "Self Esteem and Locus of Control in Minority Group Adolescents." *Educational Research*, 20, (1).

MacDonald, J.M. (1971). *Rape Offenders and Their Victims*. Springfield, IL: Charles C. Thomas.

Malamuth, N. (1981). "Rape Proclivity Among Males." *Journal of Social Issues*, 37, (4), 138-157.

Martinez, C. (1983, January 14). *Acquaintance Rape: In Happens*. Bruin News.

Muehlenhard, C., and McFall, R. (1981). "Dating Initiation from a Woman's Perspective." *Behavioral Therapy*, 12, 682-691.

Muuss, E. (1975). *Theories of Adolescence*. New York: Random House.

Openshaw, D.K., Thomas, D.L., Rollings, B.C. (1984). "Parental influences of Adolescent Self Esteem." *Journal of Early Adolescence*, 4, (3), 259-274.

Parrot, A. (1987, November) *Using Improvisational Theater Effectively in Acquaintance Rape Prevention Programs on College Campuses*. Paper presented at the 1987 Annual Meeting for the Society for the Scientific Study of Sex Convention, Atlanta, GA.

Parrot, A. (1985). *Comparison of Acquaintance Rape Patterns Among College Students in a Large Co-Ed University and a Small Women's College*. A paper presented at the 1985 National Society for the Scientific Study of Sex Convention, San Diego, California.

Parrot, A.L. and Lynk, R. (1983). *Acquaintance Rape in a College Population*. A paper presented at the 1983 National

American Associatoin of Sex Educators, Counselors, and Therapists Convention, Chicago, Illinois.

Phares, E.J. (1976). *Locus of Control in Personality.* Morristown, N.J.: General Learning Press.

Rada, R.T. (1975). "Alcohol and Rape." *Medical Aspects of Human Sexuality*, 9, (3).

Rapaport, K. and Burkhart, B.R. (1984). "Personality and Attitudional Characteristics of the Sexually Coercive Male." *Journal and Abnormal Psychology.* 93. (2), 216-221.

Rosenberg, M. (1979). *Conceiving the Self.* New York: Basic Books.

Rotter, J.B. (1966). "Generalized Expectancies for Internal versus External Control of Reinforcement." *Psychological Monographs.* 80, (1), 609.

Russell, D.E.H. (1975). *The Politics of Rape.* New York: Stein & Day.

Russell, D.E.H. (1984). *Sexual Exploitation: Rape, Child Sexual Abuse, and Workplace Harassment.* Beverly Hills, Sage.

Schwendinger, J., and Schwendinger, H. (1974). "Rape myths: In Legal, Theoretical, and Everyday Practice." *Crime and Social Issues.* 1, 18-26.

Skelton, C.A., and Burkhart, B.R. (1980). *Criminal Justice and Behavior*, 7, (2); 229-236.

Stephens, M.W. (1973). *Parental behavioral antecedents, cognitive correlates, and multidimesionality of locus of control in young children. In recent developments in research on locus of control in children and young adults.* Symposium presented at the American Psychological Association Convention, Montreal, Canada.

Thomas, G.L., Gecas, V., Weigert, A., and Rooney, E. (1974). *Family Socialization and the Adolescent.* Lexington, MA: Lenington Books.

Thomas, S. (1983). "Is Self Esteem a Masculine Characteristic?" *Journal of Educational Equity and Leadership*, 3, (1), 29-37.

Walters, J.; McKellar, A.; Lipton, M.; and Karme, L. (1981). "What Are the Pros and Cons of Co-ed Dorms?" *Medical Aspects of Human Sexuality*, 15, (8), 48-55.

Weis, K. and Borges, S. (1975). "Victimology and Rape: The Case of the Legitimate Victim." In L. Schultz (Ed.), *Rape victimology*. Springfield, IL: Charles C. Thomas.

Zellman, G., Johnson, P., Giarrusso, R., and Goodchilds, J.D. (1979, September). *Adolescent Expectations for Dating Relationships: Consensus and Conflict Between the Sexes.* A paper presented at the American Psychological Association Conference in New York, New York.

(1988). *Penal Law of New York State.* Fresh Meadows, New York: William J. McCullough.

PART II

ACQUAINTANCE RAPE PREVENTION MANUAL

12
ACQUAINTANCE RAPE PREVENTION MANUAL FOR TRAINERS

Community education about acquaintance rape and sexual assault is essential, yet extremely difficult. Several factors account for the difficulty. First, although stranger rape is an emotional topic, acquaintance rape is often an even more emotional topic. Second, upon serious consideration, many individuals may realize that they are at risk or have already experienced an acquaintance rape. Third, stranger rape implies that the victim has virtually no control over the crime because it is perpetrated by a total stranger; in the case of acquaintance rape, however, the victim may "contribute" by agreeing to a date or by participating in sexual activities, such as asking the man back to her apartment, kissing, or allowing the fondling of her breasts. Fourth, very little is known about acquaintance rape because it is reported much less frequently than stranger rape (F.B.I. Uniform Crime Reports, 1986).

Since acquaintance rape victims rarely report the crime, they may never seek or receive help even though the emotional aftermath of the rape may be devastating. Hughes and Sandler (1987) in "Friends Raping Friends" explain the difficulties facing an acquaintance rape victim. They are frequently not believed and understood by others. The victim's judgment is often called into question, and the victim frequently finds it is difficult to trust herself or others. Victims are often concerned about having to interact with the assailant again. They may be unsure about telling others of the event, especially the police. The feelings that stranger rape survivors frequently express, such as shame, guilt, fear, and disbelief are often very strong among acquaintance rape victims as well (Hughes and Sandler, 1987).

Educational Considerations

Human sexuality is an emotional topic which requires the group leader to take into account many general educational issues when planning any sexuality related program. Educators who lead sessions on acquaintance rape prevention must consider a number of factors to ensure successful programs.

Both male and female representation (among participants as well as facilitators) at the workshop is important to provide interaction and information about both sexes. Frequently, use of the terms "Acquaintance Rape," "Date Rape," "Sexual Abuse," or "Sexual Harassment" in the title of the presentation will prevent men or women who are at risk for acquaintance rape from attending. Possible appropriate titles which are more likely to draw a diverse group include:

- "Power Dynamics in Relationships"

- "Sexual Communication"

- "How To Become a Better Lover"

- "Who Makes the Decision About Sex In Your Relationship?"

- "I Know You Said 'No' but I Thought You Meant 'Yes'"

■ "Does 'No' Ever Mean 'Yes'?"

■ "How to Get What You Want, But Not More Than You Bargained For"

■ "Sexual Assertiveness"

When publicizing large events **DO NOT** use the terms "Acquaintance Rape," "Date Rape," or "Sexual Harassment" in the title if you want a large turnout. Whenever these terms have been used in the past the turnout has been small and those who need education on this topic do not come to the presentation. The terms: "Acquaintance Rape," "Date Rape," and "Sexual Harassment" will draw only feminists, who do not necessarily need education on this issue, and will scare away those who are at risk of becoming involved in acquaintance rapes as victims or assailants. If you want to have an article appear in the paper in advance of the presentation, make sure they **DO NOT** use any of those terms either.

Several community related considerations will influence the success or failure of any program. Participants need to know local rape statistics, local examples of acquaintance rape, publicity about rapes in the community, and the rape laws of the state to fully understand acquaintance rape, and to acknowledge that it can happen in their community. Group cohesiveness, the developmental stage of the group, and willingness of participants to communicate openly and freely in front of the other sex are important group dynamics. Characteristics of group members that will have a significant impact on the educational experience include age, maturity level, virginity status, parental status, previous sexual activity, past involvement in a rape, sex stereotypic attitudes, level of assertive behaviors, ethnic or racial composition, and political ideologies.

Parents who are present may feel helpless if they think that their children are at risk of rape on a date, especially since the "tried and true" warnings parents used to tell their children are not helpful in an acquaintance situation (such as "don't go out with strangers," "don't walk home alone late at night," "only go out with boys from 'good' families," or "say 'No' to intercourse").

These warnings have limited effect because most rapes occur between people who know each other and rapists come from all social classes.

And finally, during the course of the program, participants may redefine a past sexual experience as acquaintance rape. Although no one wants to think of him or herself as a rapist, potential rapist, rape victim, or potential rape victim, this may happen after the participants learn which behaviors constitute rape. The notion that a victim may have "contributed" to an acquaintance rape by getting drunk, wearing seductive clothing, going to a man's room, etc. can cause guilt for some participants and may be cause for others to blame them for previous rape situations.

Educational Applications

Open, honest communication must be encouraged and modeled by the group facilitators. Both male and female discussion leaders are important to facilitate sex segregated groups as well as model communication between men and women on sexual issues. Men and women should have the opportunity to learn from each other.

Gentle confrontation by facilitators that is not accusatory may provide group members with new ways of conceptualizing ideas. Group leaders must be comfortable in discussing sexuality and also must be sensitive to the fears and feelings of the group members. Counseling skills are important for group facilitators but are not essential if someone is available to take care of any crisis counseling needs which may arise. Therefore, the presence of representatives from rape crisis centers or other community counseling agencies are valuable members of the group.

Conducting workshops on acquaintance rape is an extremely difficult task. Facilitators must be knowledgeable about group dynamics, facilitation skills, rape law, human sexuality, counseling techniques, crisis intervention skills, adult education principles, and assertiveness training. Two resources which may be useful in group process and assertiveness education are:

Joining Together by Johnson and Johnson, and *Assertion Skills for Young Women* by Ginny McCarthy.

A wide variety of educational techniques and activities should be used to help maintain attention and reduce the potential for boredom. Effective activities for facilitating discussion and open communication during acquaintance rape prevention workshops include films and videos, role plays (acting out situations), values clarification activities, articles from local papers, "fishbowls" (one group discusses while the other looks on silently, then the groups are reversed), and brainstorming (group members suggest ideas without criticism).

The maturity level of the participants should be considered when deciding which method of self-disclosure to use. Teenagers will probably not be willing to admit to "socially unacceptable" behaviors or thoughts in front of potential dates. Sex segregated brainstorming can avoid this problem. If group members are mature and less likely to be concerned about peer pressure, the "fishbowl" technique is more desirable. It is also optimal to have participants respond individually to the values continuum on paper and then position themselves on an imaginary continuum on the floor to represent their feelings about a particular value statement.

Clearly defining the difference between stranger rape and other forms of rape is extremely important. Failure to identify differences early in the workshop may lead to confusion over definitions and arguments over semantics. It is essential to explain that you are conducting a workshop about interactions between acquaintances rather than strangers, and any digression to the topic of stranger rape must be redirected. Once the awareness of the group members has been increased regarding the risks of acquaintance rape, prevention strategies should be presented and discussed. Be careful not to frighten participants by telling them about risks without advising them on how to be safer.

Education about the topic should be broader than just acquaintance rape avoidance for women. Although only women may be legally considered rape victims according to some state laws, men are also vulnerable to sexual assault. In fact, approximately 10 percent of all sexual assault victims are men (U.S.C. Rape Prevention Education Program, 1982). Men and women need alternative suggestions for traditional sexual and dating behavior. Young men must be informed of the consequences of acquaintance rape and should be a target group for prevention programs. Although most rapes are heterosexual, it is inaccurate to assume that all rapes involve members of different sexes. The victim is sometimes the same sex as the assailant, though this does not make either of them homosexual. However, homosexual, bisexual, or heterosexual people may be involved in sexual assaults as either victim or assailant. It is imperative, therefore, to gear educational programs about acquaintance rape to all types of people.

Although most of the issues in acquaintance rape are similar regardless of the racial or ethnic group, there are some differences. You need to make sure all the major components of acquaintance rapes in the populations you serve are addressed in your program.

Talking To Groups About Acquaintance Rape Prevention

There is no one best way to discuss acquaintance rape prevention with groups. Each group is different in composition, need, cohesion, maturity level, educational background, motivation, and interest. An activity or approach that works with one group may be a disaster with another similar group in the same community. Therefore, it is important to learn as much as possible about each group before you select the activities and approaches. Contingency activities should be prepared and available in case a primary activity fails.

For example, if a group is composed of parents worried that their children will become rape victims (especially their daughters), then the "scare technique" (showing a frightening film of an acquaintance rape) would be the wrong choice because they are already frightened and feeling helpless. On the other hand, if you are talking to a group of teens who are operating under David Elkind's Model of Invincibility or the "Personal

Fable" ("It can't happen to me"), then a scare tactic may be an appropriate approach. If a majority of the men in the group are willing to honestly say how they feel and what they hear in the locker room, then verbal self disclosure may work well. But if they are "macho" or there are only a few men, anonymous written responses by males and females may be the best approach.

The combination of activities selected should be determined by the following considerations:

Logistical Considerations:

a. size of the group

b. length of time available for the session

c. sex of facilitators (one male and female would be ideal)

d. time of day of the session

e. media available

f. equipment available

g. size of room

Group Considerations:

a. political orientation (primarily liberal or conservative)

b. educational level

c. previous understanding of the topic

d. cohesion (how well they know each other, and work together)

e. presence of an acquaintance rape victim in the group

f. degree of honesty and openness of group members

Since all groups differ, the Chinese Menu Approach is recommended, it assumes that the goals and objectives for most groups are the same, but the ways to accomplish these will differ. Therefore, there are several activities presented for each objective (for objective A, select one activity from category A; to accomplish objective B select one activity from category B, etc.). The general objectives for most introductory groups on acquaintance rape are presented below.

Objectives

A. Understand acquaintance rape, its frequency in the community, and how it is related to force, threat of force, or coercion.

B. Explore feelings about acquaintance rape and listen to the other sex's feelings about it.

C. Explore cultural forces that contribute to the frequency and social "acceptability" of acquaintance rape and sexual assault.

D. Understand the contribution of inconsistent verbal and non-verbal communication patterns to acquaintance rape situations.

E. Identify prevention strategies and become empowered to work toward the elimination of acquaintance rape and sexual assault in your community.

Chinese Menu Approach to Leading Groups on Acquaintance Rape Prevention

No session will even begin to be effective in accomplishing the objectives stated above unless the group is willing to confront difficult issues. A group usually needs several hours to develop cohesion and a sense of trust. The key to keeping people interested for that length of time is to change the pace, pattern, and focus of the activities. A break at about the halfway point, with refreshments, may help maintain energy and interest.

Since the empowering part of any program is the section which models assertive and appropriate behavior, it is imperative that this section be presented before many audience members leave. Therefore, you must keep the audience members interested.

One way to provide them with prevention strategies is to challenge them to think of which behaviors addressed in the program could be incorporated into their repertoire of behaviors. It is very important to send them home with some written material on acquaintance rape, prevention strategies, and resources in the community because they may not have heard all of the important points of the program and may want to know more about the issue.

To determine which activities would be best, it is essential to get a "sense" of the group. Try to get group members to participate by using a non-threatening activity early in the session to which they can all relate. Non-threatening activities do not require telling intimate or personal things about yourself (like have you ever been involved in an acquaintance rape, and how do you feel about it?). Instead, they require non-personal information which is "safe" to share with others (such as have you ever seen a movie about acquaintance rape, and what was the main point of the movie?).

Since one of the most important elements in preventing acquaintance rape is assertiveness and clear communication for both men and women, all sessions should start with the ASSERTIVENESS IN OUR LIVES activity (Appendix A), a non-threatening exercise. This activity encourages communication about sex and will allow you to assess whether the group is communicative, liberal or conservative, willing to participate honestly and openly, responsive to discussion or lecture style, composed of mostly rational individuals, informed, insightful, willing to take risks, and educated. You should have already planned the logistics and should know about the obvious considerations (such as sex composition, age of group, etc.) by looking at the group. Upon completion of this activity, you should have most of the information you need to determine how to accomplish the objectives for the session.

OBJECTIVE A

Understand acquaintance rape, its frequency in the local community, and how it is related to force, threat of force, and coercion.

This section includes definitions of types of rape, a layperson's understanding of the law, and community rape statistics. This information should be made available to participants either by handouts, lecture, group discussion, or visual aids (slides, overhead projector, large easel, etc.). The DEFINITIONS sheet (Appendix B) is important to start with to ensure that the specific terms have the same meaning for participants and to avoid arguing semantics. Inform the participants that there are legal and sociological definitions for acquaintance rape and that you will be using the sociological definitions. The legal definitions vary from state to state. You may want to tell them that you do not want to discuss the law or semantics, but you do want to establish a common definition.

It's recommended that you use the term SEXUAL ASSAULT to discuss forced sex, because it includes the possibility of both men and women as victims, and also includes sodomy as a forced sex behavior. Have the state legal information available, as well as a listing of the maximum penalty for each offense. This material can be available during the breaks, or can be used as reference if a question arises. People will often try to divert the conversation to "safer" topics (like the law) when the discussion of feelings and risk groups is getting too uncomfortable. You should be alert for this type of diversion and redirect as soon as it occurs. If there are specific questions on the law, however, have the materials available for individual examination, so that you need not spend group time discussing law and being side tracked. If you are not from New

York State, prepare a layperson's understanding of the law for your state and make it available to all participants (Appendix C).

"Understanding The Law" (Appendix V) presents a layperson's understanding of New York State Law, the penalties for acquaintance rape committed at Cornell University, and agencies or organizations which may provide help to those involved in acquaintance rape on the Cornell University campus. This type of handout is important, but must be revised to reflect the laws of your state and the agencies and penalties specific to your community.

Depending on the type of group, you may decide to try to elicit information from them (for example, ask them to identify the differences between the various types of rape). This strategy is especially effective if the group has the attitude, "We already know it all." If they do know the answers, this time gives them permission to participate and has made your job easier because you will not have to supply all the answers. On the other hand, if they think they know it all but are misinformed, then you have learned that they need guidance and they have realized that they really do not "know it all."

You should provide a visual and concrete example of the number and frequency of acquaintance rapes and sexual assaults in your community either by handing out copies of an article, projecting a slide of an article, or having the director of the rape crisis center speak to the group. Many groups will dismiss the importance of the topic if you quote national or state statistics by saying "that kind of thing does not happen in our community." Bring the actual statistics from the local rape crisis center or a local newspaper article to refute the argument (Appendix D). Numbers of convictions are not as representative because acquaintance rapes are rarely brought to court so use the number of calls to the rape crisis center as a better indicator.

A good, general, and very recent film on this topic is **AGAINST HER WILL**. (Coronet/MTI Film and Video, 108 Wilmont Road, Deerfield, IL 60015, 1-800-621-2131, 1989) It is hosted by Kelly McGillis, and it is a documentary which explores the "whys" of acquaintance rape. It is best to use only segments of the film, as it is 60 minutes long. There are candid interviews with female rape victims, young male college students, security personnel, and counselors underscore the growing problem of acquaintance rape on college campuses.

CAMPUS RAPE (Rape Treatment Center, Santa Monica Hospital, 1250 Sixteenth Street, Santa Monica, CA 90404, (213) 319-4000, 1990) is a powerful film hosted by **LA Law** stars Susan Dey and Corbin Bernsen, which explores campus rape, and its impact with four college women who were assaulted on campuses throughout the country. This film provides critical information about stranger and acquaintance rape, how and where these crimes are likely to occur, the impact of sexual assault on victims, the role of alcohol and drugs in sexual assaults, and techniques students can use to prevent campus rape.

OBJECTIVE B

Explore feelings about acquaintance rape and listen to the other gender's feelings about it.

There are eight activities (Appendices E through L) that can be used in this section to accomplish this objective. They are presented from least to most threatening. In general, if the group is not willing to talk candidly in front of others, one of the first few activities should be selected. Very honest and open groups can make use of the "Fishbowl" technique (the most threatening in this section).

Some group members may object that the wording of the questions in these activities is too ambiguous. If so, explain that the questions were designed to be ambiguous to generate maximum discussion, and may be defined and answered any way they would like. The importance of these activities is to elicit comments, so the more ways the questions are viewed, the better the ensuing discussion. Be sure to have participants explain how they are defining the question when they discuss it. Group members will learn better from each other than from the facilitator, so your role here should be to facilitate, not lecture. Just be sure the group does not dwell on semantic discussions or monopolize arguments with other group members.

The SEXUAL ASSERTIVENESS QUESTIONNAIRE (Appendix E) is designed for non-assertive groups that are not willing to share information with others. Once members of the group have completed this sheet independently, you can effectively process this activity by asking probing questions about why a person would have answered any question in a non-assertive way. For example: if they responded "almost never" to telling their partner that they do not want to make love, you might ask, "Why is it so much more difficult to say 'I don't want to now' to sex than it is to say 'I don't want to now' to a meal?"

The key here is to have some group members volunteer to explain why they answered as they did. Care must be taken to draw relationships between non-assertive sexual communication and acquaintance rape. You may ask the group members to raise their hands to indicate how they answered a question to give others a general idea how the group feels.

The SEXUAL ASSERTIVENESS CONTINUUM (Appendix F) can be used in place of the previous activity. Participants may complete this individually or they can place themselves along an imaginary continuum along the floor. Their location on the continuum will be a non-verbal indication of how they feel about the statements. Ask them to identify why they are there, or simply have the group members observe the attitudes of other members in the group. A discussion of the reasons for the different placements should follow completion of the continuum.

Another activity which works well with males and females who are not comfortable talking with each other is I FEEL. . . (Appendix G). Separate men from women and give each group a large piece of paper with incomplete sentences on the top of each sheet. Ask the groups to finish each incomplete sentence with as many statements that apply. It may be necessary to have a facilitator of the same sex with the group. See the activity sheet for more detailed directions.

SEXUAL ASSERTIVENESS DRAMATIZATION (Appendix H) may be used to illustrate the difficulty most people have in applying assertive behaviors to sexual situations. Select one member of the audience from each sex to act out the role play. (The term "opposite sex" implies an adversarial relationship, therefore the term "other sex" is more appropriate in this type of presentation.) This is very effective and fun for the audience.

SEXUAL ASSERTIVENESS USING "I" STATEMENTS (Appendix I) may be used during the session but it is probably used best as a homework assignment for partners in a relationship to do in a private place. Only use it during the presentation when the group consists of couples and there is plenty of private space for each couple to try the activity.

The ACQUAINTANCE RAPE VALUES CLARIFICATION CONTINUUM (Appendix J) is a little more threatening but very effective with a heterogeneous (dissimilar group members), verbal group. Ask participants to circle the number on the continuum which best describes their feelings about the eight statements. Participants may be asked to discuss these statements while they remain seated, but try to get the entire group to get up and place themselves along an imaginary continuum line on the floor to visually represent how they feel about a given statement. Encourage them to discuss their feelings with each other and to change their position if they change their minds during the discussion. This activity can take up to an hour with a verbal group. Therefore, I suggest selecting only two or three of the most controversial items to discuss, and encourage the participants to continue discussing the other items during the break or after the session ends.

The SEXUAL BEHAVIOR OR SEXUAL ASSAULT? questionnaire (Appendix K) may be used with groups that have trouble differentiating between acceptable and unacceptable behavior. This activity can be processed as Appendix J. The behaviors described are not only considered rape, but also sexual harassment and voyeurism. Because some of the situations are set in a fraternity house, it may be especially appropriate to use with fraternity men.

CAN A GUY SAY NO? (Coronet/MI Film and Video, 108 Wilmont Road, Deerfield, Il 60015, 1-800-621-2131) is a video which depicts adolescent sexuality from a male's perspective.

The social and psychological pressures to have sex are dramatized. Both peer group and parent- teen situations are dramatized, which makes this film a good discussion starter about pressure to "go all the way" regardless of the wishes of the female.

The most threatening of the activities in this group, THE SEXUAL DYNAMICS FISHBOWL (Appendix L) will work only with a vocal and honest group. There should be fairly even numbers of both sexes represented, and no more than ten men and ten women in each fishbowl. If there are many participants, the group may be broken down into smaller sub-groups of ten men and ten women, but there should be a male and female facilitator for each fishbowl.

In this activity one gender is asked to make a small circle in the center of the room, and the other gender forms a larger circle surrounding the inside circle. Both face the center. The inside group responds to open ended questions asked by the facilitator; the outside circle may not speak during this time. This discussion should last from 5 - 10 minutes. Then the inside and outside circle switch places, and the members of the new inside circle explain how they felt when listening to the responses of the previous inside circle (5 minutes). Then the members of the new inside circle respond to new questions asked by their facilitator for 5 to 10 minutes, while the members of the outside circle listen silently. The facilitator of each group should confront members to encourage honest expression of feelings about the issues. The members of the circles then switch once again, and the new inner circle talks about how they felt when listening to the responses of the previous inner group (5 minutes).

OBJECTIVE C

Explore cultural forces that contribute to the frequency and social "acceptability" of acquaintance rape and sexual assault.

The 1987 Ann Landers article, "SAY 'NO' UNEQUIVOCALLY" (Appendix M) presents the view that if a man stops when a women says "no" after "leading him on," she should consider herself fortunate. It conveys the common attitude about a woman's responsibility to not tease a man sexually or she may deserve what she gets. It is sure to spark a lively discussion if you have both traditionally sex stereotypic members and feminists in the group.

Other possible activities are the discussion of publicly known cases and one or two of the participatory activities listed below. Remember that activities during a session should be varied by type, method of presentation, pace, and participation requirements. Too much of one kind gets tedious. Once again, the activities are presented from least threatening to most threatening.

The CULTURAL IMPLICATIONS OF NAMING THE PENIS (Appendix N) is a participatory activity which forces group members to discuss slang terms for male body parts, and the consequences of attributing a personality to the penis. It is an exciting activity which forces participants to look at cultural standards in a novel way.

The PARTY SCENARIO (Appendix O) is a discussion of an acquaintance rape at a fraternity party. This is most successfully used with fraternity or college age groups. The discussion following this reading should include individual rights, responsibilities of the man's friends to monitor behavior in the house, responsibility of the woman and her friends to come and go in pairs or groups, consequences of alcohol in early dating interactions, and implications and consequences of ending up in an isolated place at the end of an evening.

To further explore the cultural factors associated with acquaintance rape one of the following films or videos may be shown. Choose the one most appropriate for your group.

SUGAR AND SPICE AND ALL IS NOT NICE (Coronet/MI Film and Video 108 Wilmont Road, Deerfield, IL 60015, 1-800-621-2131, 1984) exposes contemporary social and cultural influences, including advertising and pornography, that seem to encourage the brutalization of women in our society.

Rape victims and counselors express their frank opinions about violent crimes against women and what needs to be done to stop them.

JUST ONE OF THE BOYS (O.D.N. Productions, 76 Varrick Street, New York, NY, 10013, 212-431-8923, 1978) depicts an insecure teenage male who is being pressured by his basketball team mates to participate in a gang acquaintance rape. He is not sure if he should participate or stop it. If he tries to stop it, everyone will think that he is not a "stud." This eight minute film is appropriate for high school or parent audiences. The topics raised in the film are stereotypes, reputations, peer pressure, social responsibility, alcohol, and popularity. The four films in the O.D.N. series (others listed below) were produced in 1978, so the hairstyles and clothes are dated.

SOMEONE THAT YOU KNOW (Dystar Television, Simon and Shuster, 420 Academy Drive, Northbrook, IL, 60062, 312-940-1260, 1986) opens with a very disturbing stranger rape and then progresses to presenting acquaintance rape situations, most involving physical violence. Since violence is unusual in acquaintance rape situations, this film may reinforce rape myths. The emotional trauma of rape is well documented by the victims and experts in the film. Because of its disturbing nature, this film should only be used by skilled facilitators and counselors should be available to deal with any group members emotionally disturbed by the film.

NOT ONLY STRANGERS (Centron Films, 1621 W. 9th, Box 687, Lawrence, KS, 66044) is appropriate for college or adult audiences. This film is about 25 minutes long, and raises three main issues: the cultural standards that contribute to an acquaintance rape (part 1), the decision to report (part 2), and the interaction with the legal system following the rape (part 3). Avoid showing the third part because it allows the group to dwell on the pitfalls of the legal system and avoid focusing on the reason for the rape or the concerns about reporting. The first two sections of the film are the most powerful and would be most helpful in educating about prevention. The third section could be useful at a later date when discussing the importance of what to expect when reporting a rape. This film has an extremely strong emotional impact and any acquaintance rape survivors in the audience may become disturbed by the film. If so, have a counselor or representative from the local rape crisis center on hand for personal counseling. The clothes and setting of this film is dated.

SEXUAL ASSAULT CRIMES (Human Relations Media, 175 Tompkins Avenue, Pleasantville, NY, 10570, 914-769-7496, 1987) is a filmstrip appropriate for high school or junior college audiences. The first part depicts the cultural factors which lead to sexual victimization and the second deals with prevention strategies and is more effectively used with Objective E.

IT STILL HURTS (Auburn University available from Campus Crime Prevention Programs, P.O. Box 204, Goshen, KY, 40026, 502-588-6111). is a video that portrays a date rape scenario, and then an actual interview with a woman who was raped by men whom she believed were friends. The psychological consequences and betrayal of trust that results from acquaintance rape are the main focus of this video which is most appropriate for college audiences or parent groups.

WITHOUT CONSENT (Chapman College Film and Video, 2801 Colorado Avenue, Santa Monica, CA, 90404, 800-421-2304, 1987) is a video showing the development of a relationship between Mike and Laura, two college students. It ends explosively when Mike pushes Laura too far, and they have sex without her consent. This is a dramatization of a student's actual experience and it depicts the reality of date rape and challenges the viewers to consider how it happens and who is responsible.

BETTER SAFE THAN SORRY - PART III (Film Fair Communications, 10900 Ventura Boulevard, P.O. Box 1728, Studio City, CA, 91604, 213-877-3191, 1985) is a videotape which depicts acquaintance rape as well as several other types of sexual assaults. This is appropriate for high school audiences.

DATE RAPE - WHAT COULD HAPPEN? (University of Arizona Police Department, 1331 East Fifth Street, Tuscon, AZ, 85721, 602-621-1484, 1987) is a videotape with two parts. The first part depicts a date rape following a couple meeting, drinking, and dancing at a bar. They go back to his apartment for some wine where he comes on "too strong." When she becomes uncomfortable and wants to leave, he gets angry and rapes her. In the second part, police officers provide basic information and suggestions to prevent acquaintance rape and what to do if you have been raped.

SEXUAL ASSAULT - A CHANCE TO THINK (University of Maryland Police Department, College Park, MD, 20742, 301-454-5993, 1984) is a videotape that focuses on reporting sexual assaults. It depicts the most commonly reported sexual assaults on the College Park Campus, including a rape situation.

WAKING UP TO RAPE (Women Make Movies, 225 Layfayette Street, Suite 212, New York, NY, 10012, 212-925-0606, 1985) is a film made for women by women, focusing on three female rape victims. Public attitudes toward these victims are presented as part of the problem. Although rape is often psychologically devastating, the film makes the excellent point that rape, like any trauma, can also be a catalyst for positive life changes.

RETHINKING RAPE (Stanford University, Contact "Rethinking Rape" C/O Jeanne Le Page, 171 Old La Honda Rd., Woodside, CA, 94062, 415-723-2300). is a film that was developed in conjunction with a student run Rape Education Project. It consists of six interviews with female rape victims, and an interview with a male student who was once tempted to become an acquaintance rapist. It is most appropriate for college audiences or parent groups.

HOLD ME UNTIL MORNING by Daniel Rudman from The Men's Survival Resource Book: On Being a Man In Today's World (1978), by C. Cooke (MRSB Press, Minneapolis, MN) is a funny, provoking, frustrating, and depressing script of a play that narrates an imaginary conversation a man has with his penis when it won't cooperate with his wishes. This play requires three actors, about 30 minutes, and it includes frank and suggestive language. This would only be appropriate for a very liberal audience which is willing to confront many important and difficult issues contributing to our cultural acquaintance rape mentality, such as women as objects, men being mandated to initiate sex, men being required to have erections and give their partners pleasure, men not taking responsibility for the "actions" of their penises, masturbation being "bad," and worry about what others will think about not having a date.

OBJECTIVE D

Understand the contribution of inconsistent verbal and non-verbal communication patterns to acquaintance rape situations.

The song, **LANGUAGE OF LOVE** (Appendix P), by Dan Fogelberg is the least threatening activity in this section. It describes the "games" people play when discussing sexuality with partners. This song is most useful if the participants are able to hear the song while reading the lyrics from a handout or a projection of the words on a screen. Participants should be asked if they have experienced this pattern of communication; if so, how do they feel about it? What are the consequences of this type of communication pattern? Can it ever lead to acquaintance rape or forced sex? How would they like to communicate about sex with potential partners?

The video **STOP DATE RAPE! - Part I** (Cornell University Audiovisual Center, 8 Research Park, Ithaca, NY, 14850-1247, 607-255-2090, 1987) production which shows an acquaintance rape taking place in a fraternity after heavy drinking. Peer pressure, sex role stereotypes, miscommunication, lack of assertiveness, and exploitative behavior are all depicted. The resulting rape is unexpected and unsettling. The videotape provides a very good stimulus for discussing the problems which lead to acquaintance rape and the behaviorally specific suggestions which may help to prevent acquaintance rapes.

I KNOW YOU SAID NO BUT I THROUGH YOU MEANT YES (Cornell University Audiovisual Center, 8

Research Park, Ithaca, NY, 14850-1247, 607-255-2090, 1989) is the high school version of STOP DATE RAPE. The actors are younger, and the examples and strategies for prevention are age appropriate to the high school audience.

The film **THE PARTY AND THE DORM** (Available from Cigus Vanni, Assistant Dean of Students, Swarthmore College, Swarthmore, PA, 19081, 215-328-8364, 1984) is student produced and includes two vignettes, one on acquaintance rape and one on acquaintance rape prevention. Each vignette is about 10 minutes long and provides considerable material for discussion. This resource is appropriate for high school or college students.

The 16 mm film **THE PARTY GAME** (O.D.N. Productions, 76 Varrick Street, New York, NY, 10013, 212-431-8923, 1978) shows how easily ineffective communication can lead to acquaintance rape. She wants affirmation of her attractiveness, he wants casual sex. Their misunderstanding leads to a frightening encounter. This 7 minute film is very effective for teenagers or parent groups. After viewing, the audience should discuss questions such as: What should be done to/for her? What should be done to/for him? What rights were violated in their interaction? This film elicits strong emotional reactions in viewers. Be sure to deal with the emotions before going on to discuss the content.

The 16mm film **THE DATE** (O.D.N. Productions, 76 Varrick Street, New York, NY, 10013, 212-431-8923, 1978) depicts a young black couple (he is 19, she is 15) returning to her house after a date. She is giving unintentional, non-verbal messages. He feels that she owes him sex because he paid for an expensive evening. Their interaction ends in his forcing her to comply with his wishes to "treat him like a real man." Appropriate for high school and parent groups, the film addresses issues such as parental responsibility, inconsistent verbal and non-verbal messages, age differences in dating leading to differences in expectations, and "macho" and "feminine" stereotypes. This film may be too disturbing for some groups who feel powerless (not able to control their situation or environment). Small and large group discussions should follow this film, be sure to discuss the emotions elicited by this film before discussing the content of the film.

The **ROLE REVERSAL EXPERIENCE** (Appendix Q) is a very effective tool to elicit feelings among participants first hand rather than in reaction to a film. Participants are asked to take the opposite role to that which they usually take in a dating situation (passive person or initiator). This activity will only work well with a group which is willing to risk and which trusts you as a leader. If you can carry this activity out well, it may be the most effective activity of the session by enabling participants to really experience a feeling.

It is important to refrain from using the terms "opposite sex," "males," and "females" to imply possible sex partners. Approximately 10 percent of the population is gay, and if gay individuals are in your group, they will feel excluded by the use of the term "opposite sex." It's best, therefore, to refer to the "opposite perspective" in a dating interaction.

OBJECTIVE E

Identify prevention strategies and become empowered to work toward the elimination of acquaintance rape and sexual assault in your community.

The easiest, and probably least effective, way to accomplish this goal is to distribute copies of ACQUAINTANCE RAPE AWARENESS AND PREVENTION STRATEGIES FOR MEN AND WOMEN (Appendix R). If this is all that is done in this section, the items on the list should be discussed in the large group or in small groups for clarification. Group members should be asked to add any other strategies which they think should be on the list. Ask each participant to make a contract with himself or herself to attempt incorporating at least one new prevention behavior within the next few weeks.

STOP DATE RAPE! - Part II (Cornell University Audiovisual Center, 8 Research Park, Ithaca, NY, 14850-1247, 607-255-2090, 1987) is the follow up to STOP DATE Rape -

PART I (see Objective D). This videotape presents the same scene depicted in Part I, but in Part II Mary is much more assertive and behaves in ways to decrease the vulnerability she experiences in Part I. David's behavior changes in response to Mary's assertiveness. After a confrontation about Mary insisting on stopping their sexual encounter, they go out for coffee as friends. Part II models positive behaviors, and shows how both men and women can act differently from the often typical game playing behaviors and still be friends.

NO MEANS NO: AVOIDING DATING ABUSE (Coronet/MI Film and Video, 108 Wilmont Road, Deerfield, IL 60015 1-800-621-2131, 1988) is a video in which Lisa is nearly raped by her boyfriend. Confused by fear and inexperience, she fears that the incident may have been her fault, that if she had just "given in" her boyfriend wouldn't be so upset with her. This is an important film about acquaintance rape prevention.

RAPE PREVENTION: TRUST YOUR INSTINCTS (Coronet/MI Film and Video, 108 Wilmont Road, Deerfield, IL 60015 1-800-621-2131, 1989) is a video in which dramatic vignettes illustrate situations where women should trust their instincts, and also present a chance to practice non-violent response options which can dramatically reduce panic and fear during the initial stages of a physical confrontation.

The filmstrip **SEXUAL ASSAULT CRIMES Part II** (Human Relations Media, Pleasantville, NY, 10570, 914-769-7496, 1987) is a follow up to SEXUAL ASSAULT CRIMES Part I (see Objective C). Appropriate for high school or junior college audiences, it contains two parts: the first depicts the cultural factors which lead to sexual victimization, and the second deals with prevention strategies.

WORKING AGAINST RAPE (10 Lyon Street, #101, San Francisco, CA, 94117) is a 60 minute color videotape available in 3/4" cassettes. Through interviews, the connection between rape and socialization, and sexism and violence in our culture are examined. Strategies for coping with the problem of rape in our personal lives and on a community level are also discussed.

CAN'T YOU SEE ME?: RAPE CONSEQUENCES AND RECOVERY (WRI Education, World Research Incorporated, 11722 Sorrento Valley Road, San Diego, CA, 92121-1021, 800-972-2625, 1986) is a 20 minute videodrama with an instructional guide designed for a 45 minute presentation.

ACQUAINTANCE RAPE AWARENESS AND PREVENTION BRAINSTORM: One good way to end the session would be to have participants generate the list by brainstorming prevention strategies. They should also identify community agencies that are potential resources for future acquaintance rape prevention work and/or crisis intervention. Ideas generated by the group will be more likely to be carried out than ideas generated by the group leader, but all participants should leave with some ideas of how they can make a difference to prevent forced sex.

A 16mm film which might be helpful in this section is **THE END OF THE ROAD** (O.D.N. Productions, 76 Varrick Street, New York, NY, 10013, 212-431-8923, 1978). This 8 minute long film, depicts how assertive behavior can prevent acquaintance rape. Jinny's car breaks down on a lonely night. She accepts help from a man she vaguely knows. She firmly rejects his attempts to exploit the situation and succeeds in averting the potential assault. Following the film, prevention techniques and assertive behaviors should be discussed. This film portrays clear and effective communication by a woman and is a positive way to end a very emotionally difficult session.

If you have at least half an hour left, you may want to bring in a self defense expert to teach participants some simple and effective physical and psychological self defense techniques. The session should be viewed as an introduction to learning self defense, not all they will need to know. The value of teaching physical strategies is to show participants that they don't have to have a black belt in karate to effectively execute simple self defense techniques, to learn sensitive target areas and effective combinations of strikes and blocks, and to feel less helpless. This would work best with a small group in an open area. You should stress, however, that self defense competence requires practice and training with a certified instructor. A good book to provide more information on this topic is *Fear or Freedom* by Susan E. Smith.

A final closure activity is a summary article on acquaintance rape such as "The Date Rape Syndrome" (Appendix S), "Acquaintance Rape: Between Men and Women" (Appendix T), or "Why Nice Men Force Sex on Their Friends" (Appendix U). These may be made available to students as they leave.

Summary

Other activities may also be appropriate to facilitate thinking and honest discussion about acquaintance rape and sexual assault prevention. There is no absolute formula for which activities would work best for every group. The personality of the group must first be assessed, and appropriate activities should be selected to start where the group is and challenge the group to their maximum capability. Feel free to use your own activities or alter these so they will help you to accomplish your objectives.

The most effective way to make use of this Chinese Menu Approach to Acquaintance Rape Prevention is to become very familiar with all the activities before you begin facilitating groups on acquaintance rape prevention. This means that you should participate in all of these activities with a group of friends or colleagues before you try them on your first group. One good way to accomplish this is to gather a group of potential facilitators together and explore all the activities during training sessions. However, potential facilitators who are aware of the issues will probably respond differently than potential audiences. These differences should be taken into account when deciding which activities and media to use.

You should have multiple copies of all the handouts during any sessions you are facilitating, just in case you choose a particular activity at the last minute. In addition to the handouts, you should have newsprint, many magic markers, masking tape, a 16 mm projector with a replacement bulb, an overhead projector with a replacement bulb, an extension cord with an adaptor plug, a screen, the films, a cassette tape recorder, audio tapes of the songs, video equipment, three copies of the play, a large room, and movable chairs. The summary sheet of all the activities in this section (pages 69-70) will help you to assess which material should be ready for each session.

Be sure to have a good grasp of group dynamics and group facilitating skills before you attempt to lead a group on this topic. Know your co-facilitator, and be ready and willing to respectfully disagree in front of the group so that you model a healthy way to discuss and confront each other about sexual issues with a positive resolution. You and your co-facilitator may want to divide up the responsibilities for the session by objectives (for example, you primarily facilitate Objectives A, C, and E; your co-facilitator will be responsible for the remaining objectives).

The last portion of your session should be an evaluation so that you may improve your facilitation skills and the learning of future groups. An open ended evaluation gives the participants room to critique the session and the facilitators in both a positive and negative way. A simple evaluation instrument could contain the following four incomplete sentences:

The things I liked best about this session were...

The things I liked least about this session were...

The most important thing I learned during this session was...

Please change...

Remember, you can please some of the people all of the time, and all of the people some of the time, but you cannot please all of the people all of the time. Do not worry if you get some negative comments; this material is likely to make some people very uncomfortable. Always make sure you read and pay attention to the general trends in the evaluations, and use this information to change your plan before the next session.

Finally, you have a responsibility to your group not to dredge up uncomfortable feelings and then leave them to grapple with those feelings on their own. You should be sure to provide participants with names, addresses, and phone numbers of referral agencies, such as the local Rape Crisis Centers, therapists, or counseling centers. You should also provide them with the phone number of the police and any special sexual assault task force representatives who are sensitive to acquaintance rape situations.

You are a participant in a very important process — to empower others with the ability to make a difference in their interpersonal and sexual interactions. You should be proud of the valuable contribution you are making.

Congratulations on your involvement, and good luck! Please let me know how these activities work with groups in your community. I will use your information to revise the activities and training manual to make it more effective for others.

Andrea Parrot, Ph.D.
Department of Human Service Studies
N132 MVR Hall
Cornell University
Ithaca, New York 14853
(607) 255-2512

13
MEDIA RESOURCES

A QUESTION OF CONSENT - RAPE
Woroner Films, Inc.
Coronet/MI
108 Wilmot Road
Deerfield, IL 60015
(312) 940-1260

AGAINST HER WILL
Coronet/MI Film and Video
108 Wilmont Road
Deerfield, IL 60015
(312) 940-1260
1989
60 minutes
Video $495, Rental $75

BETTER SAFE THAN SORRY - PART III
Film Fair Communications
10900 Ventura Boulevard
P.O. Box 1728
Studio City, CA 91604
(213) 877-3191
1985
19 minutes
$40.00 3 day rental

CAMPUS RAPE
Rape Treatment Center
Santa Monica Hospital Medical Center
1250 Sixteenth Street
Santa Monica, CA 90404
213-319-4000
1990
20 minutes
$50 purchase

 CAN A GUY SAY NO?
Coronet/MI
108 Wilmot Road
Deerfield, IL 60015
(312) 940-1260
1988
32 minutes
Video $250, Rental $75

CAN'T YOU SEE ME?: RAPE CONSEQUENCES AND
RECOVERY
World Research Incorporated
11722 Sorrento Valley Road
San Diego, CA 92121-1021
(619) 456-5278
1986
20 minutes
$24.50 rental

DATE RAPE - WHAT COULD HAPPEN?
University of Arizona Police Department
Sergeant Brian Seastone
1331 East Fifth Street
Tucson, AZ 85721
(602) 621-1484
1987
17 minutes
$25.00 purchase

I KNOW YOU SAID NO BUT I THOUGHT YOU SAID YES
Cornell University Audiovisual Center
8 Research Park
Ithaca, NY 14850-1247
(607) 255-2090
1989
20 minutes
Video $225, Rental $50

IT STILL HURTS
Campus Crime Prevention Program
Dan Keller
P.O. Box 204
Goshen, KY 40026
(502) 588-6111

NO MEANS NO!: AVOIDING DATE ABUSE
Coronet/MI
108 Wilmot Road
Deerfield, IL 60015
(312) 940-1260
1988
19 minutes
Video $365, Rental $75

NOT ONLY STRANGERS
Centron Films
1621 West 9th, Box 687
Lawrence, KS 66044

RAPE PREVENTION: TRUST YOUR INSTINCTS
Coronet/MI
108 Wilmot Road
Deerfield, IL 60015
(312) 940-1260
1989
18 minutes
Video $395, Rental $75

RETHINKING RAPE
Stanford University
c/o Jeanne LePage
171 Old La Honda Road
Woodside, CA 94062
(415) 723-2300

SEXUAL ASSAULT CRIMES PART I AND II
Human Relations Media
175 Tompkins Avenue
Pleasantville, NY 10570
(914) 769-7496
1987
30 minutes
purchase or 30 day free preview

SEXUAL ASSAULT - A CHANCE TO THINK
University of Maryland Police Department
Corporal Cathy Atwell
(301) 454-5993
1984
30 minutes
$60.00 two week rental, $150.00 purchase

SOMEONE THAT YOU KNOW
Dystar Television
Simon and Shuster
420 Academy Drive
Northbrook, IL 60062
(312) 940-1260
1986
30 minutes
$125.00 for 3 day rental

STOP DATE RAPE - PART I AND II
Cornell University Audiovisual Center
8 Research Park
Ithaca, NY 14850-1247
(607) 255-2090
1987
23 minutes
$50.00 3 day rental; $225.00 purchase

SUGAR AND SPICE AND ALL IS NOT NICE
Coronet/MI
108 Wilmot Road
Deerfield, IL 60015
(312) 940-1260
1984
19 minutes
Video $250, Rental $75

THE PARTY and THE DORM
Cigus Vanni, Assistant Dean of Students
Swarthmore College
Swarthmore, PA 19081
(215) 328-8364
1984
15 minutes (1 film in 2 parts)
$25.00 preview, $200.00 purchase

THE PARTY GAME
THE DATE
THE END OF THE ROAD
JUST ONE OF THE BOYS
O.D.N. Productions
76 Varrick Street
New York, NY 10013
(212) 431-8923
1978
each film about 15 minutes
$125.00 a week rental

VOICES OF POWER
Audiovisual Center
Indiana University
Bloomington, IN 474001
(812) 335-8087
1987
47 minutes
$35.00

WAKING UP TO RAPE
Women Make Movies
225 Lafayette Street
Suite 212
New York, NY 10012
(212) 925-0606
1985
35 minutes
$60.00

WITHOUT CONSENT
Pyramid Film and Video
2801 Colorado Avenue
Santa Monica, CA 90404
(800) 421-2304
1987
25 minutes
$65.00 3 day rental

WORKING AGAINST RAPE
10 Lyon Street, #101
San Francisco, CA 94117
60 minutes

TV Commercial for young men about acquaintance rape
prevention
Gail Abarbanell
Rape Treatment Center
Santa Monica, CA 90401
$250.00 per year to make and use as many copies as you want

Related Films of Interest

A QUESTION OF CONSENT - RAPE (Woroner Films, Inc., Coronet/MI 108 Wilmot Road, Deerfield, Illinois, 60015). This film is set in a court room and deals with the legal ramifications of rape.

VOICES OF POWER (Audiovisual Center, Indiana University, Bloomington, Indiana, 47401). This video describes the healing process after rape by dramatizing the interactions of six women in a support group setting. Four are victims, two are counselors; all have been deeply affected by sexual assault. This is a 1987 production, 47 minutes.

14
Chinese Menu Approach To Acquaintance Rape Prevention

Summary Sheet

Activity	Objective	Age	What needed	How sensitive	Required
INTRODUCTION					
Assertiveness in Our Lives Appendix A	Intro	All	nothing	–	Yes
OBJECTIVE A					
Definition sheet Appendix B	A	All	copies for all	–	Yes
Your State Penal Law Appendix C	A	All	1 copy	–	Yes
Local Article on AR Statistics Appendix D	A	All	1 copy or transparency OP	*	Yes

Summary Sheet

Activity	Objective	Age	What needed	How sensitive	Required
Against Her Will	A	All	video	+	No
Campus Rape	A	All	video	+	No

OBJECTIVE B

Activity	Objective	Age	What needed	How sensitive	Required
Sexual Assertiveness Questionnaire - Appendix E	B	A	copies for all	*	No
Sexual Assertiveness Continuum Appendix F	B	All	copies for all	*	No
I Feel... Appendix G	B	All	newsprint markers	*	No
Sexual Assertivenss Dramatization Appendix H	B	All	1 copy	–	No
Sexual Assertiveness Using "I" Statements, Appendix I	B	All	copies for all	*	No
Can A Guy Say No?	B	T,A	video	+	No
AR Values Clarification Continuum - Appendix J	B	All	copies for all	*	No
Sexual Behavior or Sexual Assault, Appendix K	B	C,A	copies for all	*	No
The Fishbowl Appendix L	B	All	1 copy	+	No

OBJECTIVE C

Activity	Objective	Age	What needed	How sensitive	Required
Ann Landers - Say "No" Unequivocally, Appendix M	C	All	1 copy	*	No
Cultural Implications of Naming Penis, Appendix N	C	All	Newsprint markers	*	No
Party Scenario Appendix O	C	All	nothing	*	No

Summary Sheet

Activity	Objective	Age	What needed	How sensitive	Required
Sugar and Spice and All is not Nice	C	All	video	+	No
Just One of the Boys	C	T,A	film, 16mm pro.	+	No
Someone That You Know	C	C,A	film, 16mm pro.	++	No
Not Only Strangers	C	C,A	film, 16mm pro.	+	No
Sexual Assault Crimes Part I	C	T,A	filmstrip projector	*	No
It Still Hurts	C	C,A	video	+	No
Waking Up To Rape	C	All	video	+	No
Rethinking Rape	C	C,A	video	+	No
Without Consent	C	C,A	video	+	No
Better Safe Than Sorry Part III	C	All	video	*	No
Date Rape What Can Happen	C	All	video	*	No
Sexual Assault: A Chance to Think	C	All	video	*	No
Hold Me Until Morning ***	C	C,A	play, 3 copies	++	No

OBJECTIVE D

Activity	Objective	Age	What needed	How sensitive	Required
Language of Love Appendix P	D	All	copies for all, tape, recorder	–	No

Summary Sheet

Activity	Objective	Age	What needed	How sensitive	Required
STOP DATE RAPE - Part I	D	All	video	*,+	No
I Know You Said No - but I Thought You Meant Yes	D	T	video	+	No
The Party and the Dorm	D	All	video	*,+	No
The Party Game	D	T,A	film, 16 mm pro.	*,+	No
The Date	D	T,A	film, 16 mm pro.	*,+	No
Role Reversal Experience Appendix Q ***	D	All	nothing	+	No

OBJECTIVE E

Activity	Objective	Age	What needed	How sensitive	Required
AR Awareness & Prevention - Appendix R	E	All	copies for all	–	No
No means NO!	E	All	video	+	No
Rape Prevention: Trust Your Instincts	E	All	video	+	No
STOP DATE RAPE Part II	E	All	video	–	No
Sexual Assault Crimes Part II	E	All	filmstrip projector	*	No
Working Against Rape	E	C,A	video	+	No
Can't You See Me?: Rape Consequences and Recovery	E	C,A	video	+	No
Agency & Prevention Brainstorm	E	All	newsprint & markers	–	No
End of the Road	E	All	film, 16 mm pro.	*	No

Summary Sheet

Activity	Objective	Age	What needed	How sensitive	Required
Self Defense Clinic	E	All	Self defense instructor needed	+	No
Date Rape Syndrome Articel - Appendix S	Summary	All	copies for all	–	No
Vital Signs Article Appendix T	Summary	All	copies for all	–	No
Why Nice Men Force Sex on Their Friends Appendix U	Summary	All	copies for all	–	No
Understanding the Law Appendix V	Summary	All	copies for all	–	No

AR = Acquaintance Rape
Age: **A** = Adult, **C** = College Age, **T** = Teenager
What Needed: **OP** = overhead projector; **16 mm pro.** = 16 mm projector
How Sensitive: – = minimum; * = moderate; + = maximum
*** = difficult to process

OBJECTIVES:

A - Understand acquaintance rape, its frequency in the community, and how it is related to force, threat of force, or coercion.

B - Explore feelings about acquaintance rape and listen to the other sex's feelings about it.

C - Explore cultural forces that contribute to the frequency and social "acceptability" of acquaintance rape and sexual assault.

D - Understand the contribution of inconsistent verbal and non-verbal communication patterns to acquaintance rape situations.

E - Identify prevention strategies and become empowered to work toward the elimination of acquaintance rape and sexual assault in your community.

Appendix A

ASSERTIVENESS IN OUR LIVES
(Time necessary depends on group size, 10 to 30 minutes)

Introduction:

Introduce the session by using a non-threatening example which relates to assertiveness but does not reduce discomfort associated with a discussion of sexuality. This is an example which relates to smoking in an elevator. Tell participants the following:

Imagine you are all non smokers who hate cigarette smoke.

You are waiting for an elevator on the first floor, and you must ride to the third floor. When it arrives you get on it and so does someone with a lit cigarette.

WHAT DO YOU DO? (try to elicit as many different responses as possible from the participants).

WOULD YOUR RESPONSE BE DIFFERENT IF THERE WERE A "NO SMOKING" SIGN IN THE ELEVATOR?

WOULD YOUR RESPONSE BE DIFFERENT IF THIS PERSON WERE YOUR SUPERVISOR OR TEACHER?

PROCESSING:

The responses probably ranged from very non-assertive (such as I would hold my breath, or I would get off the elevator and walk), to aggressive (such as cigarettes are disgusting, or I would put it out for him or her), to lying (such as I am allergic to cigarette smoke). Did the types of responses differ by sex? If so why?

Most likely, very few answers were assertive, and would not fit into the formula of: "When you do 'x', I feel 'y', and I want you to do 'z'." Assertions are difficult with people we do not know, but may even be more difficult with people we know.

There are several reasons why it is even more difficult to be assertive in a sexual interaction:

1. You must put your desires over those of someone you care about when you are asserting for something contrary to the desires of others.

2. You are not usually taught or encouraged to talk about sex or use sexual words in normal conversation.

3. Communication about sex often takes place in the context of "game playing," not honest communication about feelings.

4. We are not generally expected to share our feelings with others, especially if that sharing may make us vulnerable.

5. We may not be absolutely sure about what we want sexually.

6. We have been receiving conflicting messages from many different sources in our lives about what is correct and how we should behave sexually.

7. We can use the law or our health as reasons to be assertive about smoking because smoking may be hazardous to health and is illegal in some non ventilated public areas. It is not always illegal or unhealthy to engage in behaviors such as "petting."

8. Either men or women are allowed to dislike smoking, but neither sex is supposed to dislike sex, and each sex is bound by certain restrictive sex roles.

Appendix B

DEFINITIONS

RAPE - Penis-vagina intercourse against a woman's will and without her consent (this is a legal definition, and varies slightly by state).

ACQUAINTANCE RAPE - Rape by someone the victim knows.

DATE RAPE - Rape by someone the victim has been or is dating.

SOFT RAPE - Coercion used to engage a victim in intercourse against his/her will.

CONSENTUAL SEX - sexual relations with both partners desiring sex.

SIMPLE RAPE - rape without violence or force, with a single assailant or without any other accompanying crime (kidnapping, murder, assault, etc.)

AGGRAVATED RAPE - rape which occurs with more than one assailant or in conjunction with another crime (kidnapping, murder, assault, etc.)

SEXUAL ASSAULT - A forced sexual act against one's will (men or women may be assaulted according to this definition).

Note: Victims in approximately 10 percent of all sexual assault cases are men.

Appendix C

NEW YORK STATE PENAL LAW

Forcing or coercing someone to have sexual intercourse or to engage in other sexual contact is against the law. Specifically, if a woman is forced to have sexual intercourse or if she is unable to consent, the behavior of the perpetrator is considered first degree rape. The force necessary can be any amount or threat of physical force which places the woman in fear of injury or in fear for her life. The perpetrator does not need to use a weapon or to beat her to make her fearful of injury or for her life.

She is considered unable to consent if she is mentally incapacitated or is physically helpless due to drug or alcohol consumption, is mentally defective, is asleep, or is less than 17 years of age. If a female has intercourse under these circumstances, it is rape.

Forcing or coercing a man or a woman to engage in any sexual contact other than sexual intercourse under the circumstances mentioned above is considered second or thrid degree rape, sexual abuse or sodomy.

30 Rape Reports Made This Year

Several Incidents Recently

By HEATHER MARTENS

Ithaca Rape Crisis and the Tompkins County Sheriff's Department reported 30 instances of rape or attempted rape in the Ithaca area from January to June this year. Several have already been reported in September, the agencies said.

Ithaca Rape Crisis alone received 27 calls during the first six months of this year, according to Lynn M. Harllee '84 of the center.

Twenty of the cases were rapes and the other seven were attempted rapes or instances of sexual abuse, Harllee said. Of the total, 13 were reported to law enforcement agencies, she added.

Seventy-five percent of the rapes were acquaintance rapes, she said, but "that doesn't mean that Ithaca is immune to stranger rapes."

"Many women don't think stranger rape happens in Ithaca. Unfortunately, it does," an Ithaca Rape Crisis representative said.

The Ithaca Police Department reported two actual rapes during the month of July, according to Sgt. David Barnes.

The Tompkins County Sheriff's Department has handled one case in September.

Safety Measures

In a joint press release, Tompkins County Sheriff's Department and Ithaca Rape Crisis recommended several safety measures:

• Don't open doors to strangers; ask for identification from service personnel, and consider installing a one-way viewer.

• Don't leave keys in outdoor niches.

• Use your initials, not your first name, in phone books and on

30 Rapes Reported In Ithaca This Year

Continued from Page 1

mailboxes.

• When traveling in your car, make sure all doors are locked, and lock doors when you leave your car. Have your keys ready as you approach the car, and always check the back seat.

• When walking on the street be aware of the behavior of others. If you're being followed go to a nearby house or business that's open, or turn and walk in the opposite direction. Remember places in the area that are open at night.

• Avoid walking alone at night and use caution in or circumvent deserted areas. Let someone know where you're going and when you'll return. Walk with confidence, but be prepared to scream if necessary.

• Hitchhiking can be dangerous. Look into public transit schedules or carpooling possibilities. Don't get into a car if you're at all suspicious.

Blue Light

The Blue Light Escort Service operates from 10:30 to 12:30 nightly; call 256-7373 for an escort. The service still needs volunteers; for more information call Alexander von Gordon, 256-7406.

Ithaca Rape Crisis guarantees confidentiality and can be reached through Suicide Prevention and Crisis at 272-1616. Counselors are available 24 hours per day.

In Ithaca call the Ithaca Police Department, 272-3245.

Outside the city of Ithaca call the Tompkins County Sheriff's Department, 272-2444.

Appendix E

SEXUAL ASSERTIVENESS QUESTIONNAIRE

Directions: Check which category best indicates your response
to the questions below.

Almost Always	Sometimes	Almost Never	How often would/do you ...
_____	_____	_____	....make your own decision regarding intercourse or other sexual activity regardless of your partner's wishes.
_____	_____	_____	....use or not use birth control regardless of your partner's wishes.
_____	_____	_____	....tell your partner when you want to make love.
_____	_____	_____	....tell your partner when you don't want to make love.
_____	_____	_____	....tell your partner you won't have intercourse without birth control.
_____	_____	_____	....tell your partner you want to make love differently.
_____	_____	_____	....masturbate to orgasm.
_____	_____	_____	....tell your partner s/he is being too rough.

Almost Always	Sometimes	Almost Never	How often would/do you ...
_____	_____	_____	....tell your partner you want to be hugged or cuddled without sex.
_____	_____	_____	....tell a relative you're uncomfortable being hugged or kissed in certain ways.
_____	_____	_____	....ask your partner if s/he has been examined for sexually transmitted diseases.

Appendix F

SEXUAL ASSERTIVENESS CONTINUUM

Directions: Circle the number on the continuum to indicate the strength of your agreement with the statement on either end of the continuum.

1. In a sexual relationship if something bothers you, you should always tell your partner.

   In a sexual relationship it is better not to tell your partner if something is bothering you.

   1   2   3   4   5

2. When having sex with a new person, it is best to state what you want and don't want before you actually do anything sexual.

   When having sex with a new person it is best to allow the relationship to develop and try to non-verbally alter your partner's behaviors that you don't like.

   1   2   3   4   5

3. When would you bring up the possibility of having a sexually transmitted disease with a partner?

When making the date	Before taking clothes off	Before sex	After first sexual act	After one of you has been told you have an STD	Never

4. "No" means NO.

   "No" means maybe or yes.

   1   2   3   4   5

Appendix G

I FEEL . . .

Break into male and female groups of not more than eight people. Have each complete one or more of the following incomplete sentences on newsprint. You may put sheets on a wall with one incomplete sentence on each and have them mill around and write a statement to complete the sentences on each sheet.

Men:

I feel teased when . . .

When a woman leads me on sexually, I have the right to . . .

When a woman sends me conflicting messages where her behavior says yes and words say no, I believe . . .

When beginning a relationship, I want women to know . . .

Women:

It is difficult to express msyelf honestly in a new male/female relationship because . . .

When beginning a relationship, I want men to know . . .

I feel manipulated to have sex when . . .

I feel most degraded in a relationship when . . .

(15 minutes)

Bring the groups back together and have them read their responses and discuss them with the other sex group. How may these things lead to power abuse in a relationship? (30-45 minutes).

SEXUAL ASSERTIVENESS DRAMATIZATION

Consider the difference between the reactions elicited by each of these two situations in which assertiveness skills are applied in a dating situation where a woman initiates a conversation with a man (while shaking his hand):

Scenario 1

How do you do? I am _____ (insert a female's name), and I would like to invite you to have dinner with me. How does that sound to you?   (He will probably give an affirmative response.)

I just want you to know that I am only interested in petting above the waist for at least the first five dates, but after that I may consider sexual intercourse. Is that okay with you?   (He will probably think you are crazy.)

Ask the group what they think about that kind of assertiveness. Why does it sound so bizarre?

Scenario 2

How do you do? I am _____ (insert a female's name), and I would like to invite you to have dinner with me. How does that sound to you?   (He will probably give an affirmative response.)

I really love Chinese food but I am not so hot on Mexican food. Would it be alright with you if we went to the little Chinese restaurant down the street?   (Wait for his response, negotiate if necessary.)

If we are in the mood after dinner and feel like a movie, since I am a real Sylvester Stallone fan, I don't like Clint

Eastwood, could we go see "Rambo?"   (Wait for his response, negotiate if necessary.)

Ask the group how the second scenario sounded compared to the first. Why is it not acceptable for us to be assertive in sexual situations, while it is more acceptable to be assertive in non-sexual situations?

Would your reaction have been different if the man were asking the question? Why?

SEXUAL ASSERTIVENESS USING "I" STATEMENTS

Introduction

There are probably many things you like about your partner interpersonally and sexually. There are also some things you would like to change. If you don't have a partner right now, you still probably have an idea of what you would like and dislike in an interpersonal and sexual relationship.

A very difficult communication task is to let your partner know what you don't like in a way that will not cause hard feelings or anger. One way to do this is to explain that you don't like the act, but you like the person and you like many other acts performed by your partner. In addition, if you can suggest what you would like instead, your partner may not feel helpless when you say what you don't like.

It is easier to hear criticism when:

■ positive feedback is given at the same time;

■ the act, not the person is rejected;

■ the criticism does not come at a time of "high emotional investment" (for example, tell your partner at breakfast, rather than when you are making love);

■ only one criticism is given in a sitting, so the person doesn't feel like there is nothing he or she can do right;

■ the message is clear, and the verbal message matches the non-verbal message.

Directions

For short term relationships (if this is your first sexual interaction with this partner):

If you feel you can't tell your partner what you like and don't like before you begin to interact sexually, then tell him or her immediately when a behavior you don't like begins.

1.   Use the formula "When you do x, I feel y and I want you to do z."

2.   Be consistent with your verbal and non-verbal messages.

3.   Reject the behavior, not the person (for example, don't say "You are a terrible lover," or "Can't you do anything right?" But: "When you kiss my neck in that way, I feel uncomfortable and I'd like you to stop kissing my neck." Make sure the feeling you indicate is clearly negative.

4.   Do not allow the behavior to continue once you have clearly stated your displeasure with it.

5.   If your partner does not stop that behavior, ask him or her to explain what they think you said. If your partner doesn't understand, explain again using different words, and check to make sure your verbal and non-verbal messages are consistent. If he or she understands, but still will not stop, GET OUT OF THE SITUATION, your wishes are being ignored.

For long term relationships -

To be done in the session:

Make a list of the things you like and dislike about what your partner does sexually. Now circle those things in the dislike column which you really want changed, and leave the items which you could live with. Now number the circled items in the order of most important to least important ("1" being the most important).

To be done at home with your partner:

When you talk with your partner about this, have him or her make a list for you too. Then set aside a time when you will not be interrupted to discuss these issues. Tell your partner one thing from your like list, then one from your dislike list, and then finally another from your like list. When your are discussing the item from the dislike list, be specific, provide an alternate or substitute behavior, and put the dislike item in the formula of "when you do x, I feel y." (For example, "when you ask me to give you a massage, but you won't give me one afterwards, I feel exploited or unimportant, I wouldn't feel that way if you would give me a back massage too.") Then ask your partner to repeat back to you the positives, the negatives, the feelings you stated, and the suggestions you made. Once your partner has clearly heard all of what you have said, then switch roles, and your partner will tell you what he or she does not like.

Work on only one item at a time, and when you have mastered that, then go on to another one on your dislike list. Continue to revise your lists, and keep moving the improved behaviors over to your like side. This process could take months, but the results will be worth it (Parrot, 1986).

Appendix J

ACQUAINTANCE RAPE AWARENESS VALUES CLARIFICATION CONTINUUM

Directions: Circle the number on the continuum to indicate the strength of your agreement with the statement on either end of the continuum.

1. Women are never respon-   Women invite rape by their
   sible for their rapes.   actions, appearance or
                                  behavior.

      1   2   3   4   5

2. Women who have erotic   No woman wants to be raped.
   fantasies about rape   Fantasies about rape are
   want to be raped.   different than wanting to be
                                 raped.

      1   2   3   4   5

3. Wives can be raped by their   Wives can't be raped by their
   husbands.   husbands.

      1   2   3   4   5

4. Every man is a potential   Only certain types of men are
   rapist.   potential rapists.

      1   2   3   4   5

5. I find it easier to believe a   I tend to believe a woman who
   woman who fights back.   does not fight back.

      1   2   3   4   5

6. Society condones rape.   Society condemns rape.

      1   2   3   4   5

7. Rape is motivated by   Rape is motivated by a need
    sexual needs.   to overpower.

      1   2   3   4   5

8. In sex "no" means NO.   In sex "no" means maybe or
                                   yes.

      1   2   3   4   5

Appendix K

SEXUAL BEHAVIOR OR SEXUAL ASSAULT?

Directions: Circle the number on the continuum to indicate the strength of your agreement with the statement on either end of the continuum.

1. Hawkeye and Hotlips have been dating and having sexual intercourse for months. She is asleep when he arrives. She awakens after he has penetrated her.

Acceptable   Abuse

    1   2   3   4   5

2. On *Moonlighting*, Maddy told David to leave forcefully and slapped him once. He took her in his arms and kissed her. They then had sexual intercourse.

Acceptable   Abuse

    1   2   3   4   5

3. On Jack and Jill's first date they go back to his room, have a few drinks, she says no to fooling around but doesn't stop him. He won't take no for an answer. They have sexual intercourse.

Acceptable   Abuse

    1   2   3   4   5

4. In a fraternity house Wilma gets drunk and falls asleep in a brother's room because she can't get a ride home. Fred comes in and has sexual intercourse with her while she is passed out.

Acceptable   Abuse

    1   2   3   4   5

5.   A virgin fraternity pledge is required to have sexual intercourse before he can become a brother. (Consider your response based on the victimization of the pledge).

Acceptable   Abuse

     1   2   3   4   5

6.   JR asks Sue Ellen out, knowing of her reputation as a loose woman. They end up back in his room at the fraternity house for consensual sex. She stops when she sees three sets of eyes watching her from the closet. JR did not know his brothers were in the closet.

Acceptable   Abuse

     1   2   3   4   5

Appendix L

SEXUAL DYNAMICS FISHBOWL ACTIVITY

All of the men are asked to form a small circle in the center of the room, and the women will form a larger circle around the men. People in both circles face the center. Only the members of the inner circle are permitted to talk, and are asked to discuss selected questions below for approximately 10 minutes. Once the men are finished, the women go into the center, respond to how they felt about what the men said, and then they respond to the same questions for about 10 minutes. Now all members make one large group, the men have an opportunity to respond to how they felt about the women's comments. A general discussion follows.

Fishbowl Questions:

Situations in which I feel vulnerable are . . .

Cues which make me wary are . . .

I feel I have a right to sex when . . .

I feel someone is giving me a sexual come-on when . . .

I feel powerless in a relationship when . . .

(Feel free to design your own questions too.)

Appendix M

Don't Blame the Victim

If you heard about someone getting robbed, you wouldn't blame them for the crime.

If you later found out that when it happened the victim was walking alone at midnight, wearing expensive clothing and flashing cash and jewelry, you might question their sanity, but you wouldn't blame them. And when the criminal was brought to trial, the defense lawyer would never argue that the victim was asking for it.

But when the crime is rape, that's exactly what happens. The victim is blamed, and branded as a slut. Our judicial system staunchly protects the rights of defendants, without offering comparable shields to victims.

The repercussions of this trend are frightening. When a case comes to court, such as the recent case of three St. John's University students charged with rape, it seems the victim, not the accused, is on trial.

The victim is brutalized on the witness stand, forced to account for her lifestyle, her behavior, her dress. The jury may even hear how many men the victim has consensually slept with, but they are never told how many others the defendant has raped.

It's become a matter of policy for defense lawyers to launch full-blown attacks on victims. The state must prove that sexual intercourse occurred without the victim's consent. Proving that intercourse occurred is simply a matter of scientific evidence, and somewhat difficult to contest.

But the issue of consent is not as clear-cut; there's no scientific evidence, no DNA experts to offer proof. It's her word against his, and defense lawyers will go to any length to prove that her word just isn't worth much.

That the lawyers are allowed to do so is itself questionable, but what is really frightening is that juries use this "evidence" as the basis for acquittals.

And the jury did so this summer, in the trial of three men from St. John's in New York charged with the rape of a female student.

The victim endured hours of cross-examination by lawyers demanding to know what she was wearing, why she went to the party, how many drinks she had. And all three defendants were acquitted.

The defendants went home to rejoice, complaining bitterly about the disruption in their lives. But there was no celebration for the victim, whose life has been shattered.

As for the jurors, they went home to their families, the trial becoming a distant memory. They were quick to justify their verdict, arguing that it was based on the inconsistencies in the victim's testimony. For example, they said, she didn't remember how many drinks she had.

Well, gee, that's really an important issue. If they didn't find her credible, fine. But to not find

Reprinted by permission of the publisher from *The Cornell Daily Sun*, September 3, 1991.

her credible based on her failure to recollect the number of drinks she had is unjustifiable. Nothing could be more irrelevant.

No matter how many drinks she had—be it one or 10—she did not asked to be raped. It would have been surprising if she could remember. I'm not sure how many drinks I had Saturday night, and I didn't have to cope with the trauma of being forced to have sex with six men.

What happened at St. John's could happen at Cornell. So we've got to learn that no means no, that she wasn't asking for it.

No one asks to be raped; no one asks to endure the hell that victims face in our judicial system. Protect the rights of the defendants, but remember that victims have rights, too.

And that's what juries need to learn. Because we all want to live in a world that protects our freedom, a world where no means no. That's not being unreasonable; that's not asking too much. That's asking for freedom, and we are all entitled to it.

Debra Birnbaum '92 is a Sun columnist. *Inalienable Writes* **appears every other Tuesday.**

CULTURAL IMPLICATIONS OF NAMING THE PENIS

The fact that giving the penis a name is commonplace in our society and allows us to assume that the penis is a separate individual with its own wants and thinking capacity. After all, doesn't George (or what ever you have chosen to call it) get big when he gets excited, or get small when he is sore? Sometimes George becomes erect while the man is sleeping, and can't be held responsible for his thoughts. In other words, George has a mind and a personality of his own.

What are the consequences of personifying penises? If a penis is not part of the man, then the man does not have to feel responsible for the actions of the penis.

Think of the types of names penises are given. They are all male names, and usually macho male names. It is unusual to hear a penis given a name like "little Tommy"; we are more likely to hear a penis referred to as "Big John."

Objectives:

A. To get the group thinking of the implications of penis naming behavior.

B. To have the group members take some ownership for this behavior.

C. To provide participants with specific alternatives to begin to reverse the problems associated with the behavior.

Directions:

A. Give as many names as you can think of which people use to refer to the adult human penis.

1. Circle all the proper names which indicate personification.

2. Have the group help you identify those which are male names.

3. Tell them that you will not be discussing the street or slang terms for penis at this moment, but will discuss those terms later, (along with slang terms for vagina, breast, intercourse, and elbow).

B.   What are the societal implications when a penis has a separate identity from its owner?   (e.g., Is a man held accountable for his sex crime or does the penis' separate identity excuse the behavior?) Divide the large group into small co-ed groups and ask them to consider these questions:

How has our discomfort in discussing sexual parts and concepts contributed to this problem?

What can we do on an individual and social level to reverse these problems?

In the large group again, have each group share their solutions.

Discuss the following concepts:

• Personification of the penis

• "Using" people sexually

• Behavioral expectations for men and women

• Peer pressure

• Feelings about masturbation

- Mandate to have all sexual interactions culminate with intercourse

- Fear of homosexuality

- Need to be with a member of the opposite sex

- Men always having to initiate, and women having to play games

- Men fearing the enjoyment of self or other men

Sexual Term Lists

Have the group brainstorm a list of slang terms for breast, vagina, intercourse, and elbow. What kind of words were generated for each term (such as: angry, dirty, pejorative, happy, violent, passive, active, etc.)? How many words were generated for each? Why were the lists longer for some terms than others? Why were there differences?

Appendix O

PARTY SCENARIO

At a friday night party, Jane, a sophomore met Bill, a senior who lived at the house. After dancing for a few songs, Bill asked Jane if she would like a beer, and she said she would love one. They hung out by the bar talking and drinking for a couple of hours, and were finding themselves increasingly attracted to each other as time went on. Bill kept Jane's glass full of beer, and she continued to try to empty it. Late in the evening Bill suggested a "house tour." By then both of them were pretty drunk and the house tour ended at Bill's room where they continued to drink. Soon they were making out on Bill's bed, and Jane really seemed to be enjoying herself. By the time Bill finished undressing Jane, she was semi-conscious. He had intercourse with her. This was her first sexual intercourse experience.

Appendix P

LANGUAGE OF LOVE
Dan Fogelberg

She says no, but she means yes
What she wants you know that I can't guess
When we want more you know we ask for less
Such is the language of love

I say leave when I mean stay
But she don't see and so she moves away
What we really want you know we rarely say
Such is the language of love

Tooth for tooth and eye for eye
We hide our hearts and then we don't say why
Its truth for truth and lie for lie
Such is the language of love

When a love begins to wander no one ever knows
But we feel it deep inside us
Long before it shows
Long before it shows

With heavy hearts we're born to love
Words don't ever seem to say enough
But I sense the fire, a tender touch
Speaks of the language of love

When a love begins to wander no one ever knows
But we feel it deep inside us
Long before it shows
Long before it shows

She says no, but she means yes
What she wants you know that I can't guess
When we want more you know we ask for less
Such is the language of love
Such is the language of love

Reprinted by permission of the author.

ROLE REVERSAL EXPERIENCE
Adapted from the ROLE REVERSAL DATE
developed by Warren Farrell

CAUTION - This activity will only work well with those groups in which:

- There has been some trust established between the participants and the leader.

- Not all participants know each other.

- There are nearly equal numbers of males and females.

- There is at least one hour remaining to allow participants to experience the feelings elicited by the activity and to process the activity.

- The group is fairly talkative and willing to risk.

- There are some "hams" in the group.

- The facilitator is experienced in working with groups.

- There are at least 20 participants.

Objectives:

1. To provide the participants with the experience of feeling how difficult it is from the opposite perspective in a dating interaction.

2. To enable the participants to gain insight into how they may make the dating interaction less difficult.

3. To have participants learn from their feelings and each other, rather than from the facilitator.

Directions:

Participants are told that they will have an opportunity to experience the dating interaction from the opposite perspective or role which is usual for them (for example, if one is usually the aggressor, then s/he will behave passively, and vice versa).

They are told that the goal for the new aggressors is to end up with a partner at the end of the 15 minute experience. In addition, they are to establish a long range goal mentally (such as a coffee, good night kiss, petting, intercourse, etc.), and do what ever they consider most effective in attaining the long range goal.

Tell Participants:

Please do not select someone who you know. Remember, if you do not know anything about your potential partner, the only criterion you can use for assessment or interest is the initial appearance of the individual. What type of strategy will you use to attract the person in which you are interested?

The passive participants are to wait until they are approached. The reputation of the passive participants is at stake if they consent to too much too fast. Once a person's reputation is destroyed, they may have a difficult time finding someone to take care of them, and support them forever. Therefore, the passive person must attract a potential partner, but not give them "too much too soon." On the other hand, if the passive person appears too prudish, the aggressor may find another possible partner.

If there is an uneven number of aggressors and passive participants, there will be some without partners. Therefore, individuals in each group should decide what they will do in order to end up with a partner.

The participants are provided with the opportunity to now interact with each other for 15 minutes in order to end up with a partner. Some will ask what if they do not consistently behave in one way or the other, but are in the middle. Tell them that on the continuum of behaviors it is unlikely that they are EXACTLY in the middle, so they should behave in the manner which is least common for them; and if they are truly EXACTLY in the middle, they may choose either behavior.

It is important to not assume that all people in your group are heterosexual. Therefore do not refer to aggression as a traditionally male behavior, and passivity as a female behavior. Approximately 10 percent of the population is gay (homosexual), and that group will not gain any insights from this activity if they are forced to behave heterosexually.

The facilitator should not participate, but should observe the interactions.

Processing:

1. Ask participants how it felt to be in the opposite role?

2. Discuss objectifying (it is easier to be rejected by someone you do not know well, and are not "invested in"; therefore, it is less ego deflating to be rejected by a sex object rather than a person).

3. Ask which strategies were effective?

4. Ask how they felt when someone did to them what they usually do to others in a similar situation.

5. Ask what they learned about having to assume the opposite role?

6. If they had a choice, which role would they assume in real life?

7. Will their behavior change as a result of this activity? If so, how?

8. If they chose not to participate, what was the rationalization used for the refusal?

GOOD LUCK...this is an extremely difficult activity to facilitate, but one which provides participants with tremendous insights if done properly.

ACQUAINTANCE RAPE AWARENESS AND PREVENTION STRATEGIES FOR MEN AND WOMEN

Things you can do to help you reduce your risk for acquaintance rape involvement are listed below. Unfortunately, there are no guaranteed prevention strategies since every acquaintance rape situation is different. The one thing that all acquaintance rape situations have in common is that one partner (usually the male) forces the other to have sex. Therefore, you should always try to be aware of your surroundings, and try to stay out of situations where you may force another person or you may be forced to do something you don't want to do.

FOR EITHER PARTNER:

Self Assessment

1. Think about what you really want from or with that partner.

2. Be aware of stereotypes which prevent you from acting as you want to (such as a woman not being able to initiate, or a man not being able to say "no").

Personal

1. Feel good about yourself, and if you don't - get yourself involved in activities and with people who will make you feel better.

2. Get emotional help if you have been the victim of a sexual assault before, or if you feel you need help.

3. Eliminate completely or limit your alcohol and drug consumption. Most acquaintance rapes happen when one or both partners are intoxicated or high.

Communication

1.   Communicate what you really want.

2.   Say what you really are thinking.

3.   Set clear limits for acceptable behavior (such as "no petting below the waist").

Assertiveness

1.   Believe and act as if your needs are important, without exploiting others.

2.   Do not allow yourself to be put in vulnerable situations.

3.   Suggest what you would like to do on a date.

Interpersonal

1.   Pay attention to non-verbal cues.

2.   Listen to what your partner is really saying, and pay attention to the words (such as "no" means NO).

3.   View each other as equals.

Awareness

1.   Observe how the environment around you is changing (such as your being left at a party by your friends when you don't know how you will get home).

2.   Know your rights.

3.   Know which behaviors constitute rape.

FOR WOMEN:

Self Assessment

1.   Trust your instincts when you are fearful (listen to that little voice inside you and act on it).

2.   Ask yourself: "Am I able to say no if I am uncomfortable with what is happening?"

Communication

1.   Use assertive verbal confrontation if you need to (such as "I feel uncomfortable when you don't listen to me, or when you touch me like that").

2.   Mean what you say and say what you mean.

Interpersonal

1.   Do not allow others to violate your personal space.

2.   Do not assume that someone who has been non-violent in the past will be non-violent in the future.

3.   If you do not like what someone is doing to you, reject the activity, not the person.

4.   Passivity, coyness, and submissiveness are dangerous, and can create a climate in which sexual aggression may occur.

Awareness

1.   Since you can't tell who has the potential for rape by simply looking, be on your guard with every man.

Control

1. Have an escape plan from your home.

2. Control your environment.

3. Dress so you can move easily, freely, and quickly.

4. Yell "fire" (rather than "rape" or "help") if you need help.

5. Relax the rules only after you know someone well, if at all.

6. Have access to a phone.

7. Have a way to get home by yourself in each situation (cab fare, friend with a car, bus fare).

8. Pay your own way.

9. Avoid being alone with a man unless you clarify your intentions to him and are clear about his.

10. Get out of a dangerous situation as soon as you sense danger.

11. Ask repairmen or deliverymen for identification before opening the door.

12. Take assertiveness training and self defense courses.

FOR MEN:

Interpersonal

1. Use peer pressure positively to help stop abusive behaviors which may lead to acquaintance rapes (for example,

condemn, rather than condone, the behavior of a peer who has taken advantage of a sexual partner).

2.   Assume that "no" means NO. If you are right, you have not offended your partner. If you are not, your partner will have to initiate to achieve what she/he really wants.

3.   Do not exploit others sexually.

4.   Don't feel as if you always have to initiate sexually, and don't initiate if you don't want to. You are allowed to have morals too!

5.   Understand that sex doesn't necessarily mean emotional intimacy. Emotional needs are met through friendships.

6.   Listen to the messages your partner is giving.

Awareness

1.   Ask yourself if you really want to have intercourse with someone who does not want to have intercourse with you?

2.   Ask yourself how will you feel about this tomorrow if she says she never wanted to have intercourse?

3.   Understand that acquaintance rape and sexual assault are crimes.   An acquaintance rape happens if you have intercourse with a partner against her will and without her consent.

4.   Understand that most rapes happen between people who know each other.

5.   Ask yourself if you are willing to go to jail for a non-consensual sexual act?

THE DATE-RAPE SYNDROME *by Dr. Andrea Parrot*

"WHY IS THIS HAPPENING! I TRUSTED HIM!!"

ILLUSTRATION BY SUE LUNN

"Had we but world enough, and time/This coyness, lady, were no crime..."
        "To His Coy Mistress"
        by Andrew Marvell
        (1621–1678)

For far too long, women have been pressured into having sex against their wishes. Their "no's" have often been interpreted as "yes." Today, frightening new evidence is coming to light: rape is not confined to sexual assaults perpetrated

by strangers. Rather, women are being raped by men they have known, dated, and trusted.

When does a date turn into rape? In a society of changing social mores, what are the acceptable standards of sexual behavior in dating situations? As our awareness grows and people become more willing to express their feelings and discuss their experiences in relation to dating and its sexual expectations, the dating ritual is coming under close examination.

Differing expectations are major reasons for the prevalence of date or acquaintance rape. Family, peer group, religion, ethnic group, and geographic region all contribute to the establishment of criteria for acceptable sexual behavior on a date. Yet these criteria often conflict. Generation by generation, and location by location, expectations shift and are redefined. As a result, very confusing messages are given by both women and men on dates. One outcome of this ineffective communication is acquaintance rape.

According to traditional dating patterns, a man initiates the social interaction by asking a woman out for an evening of entertainment. He is expected to show her a good time and to pay all of the expenses. The time and frequency a couple has been dating are expected to correlate with the degree of intimacy the woman will allow. Often, dating is seen as the first step toward courtship and marriage. But while the woman may stress the permanent bond, the man may be more interested in a less serious involvement. This conflict gives the interaction a game-like quality, in which both partners may be dishonest about the goals they are pursuing.

But what happens when a woman initiates the invitation? Of 106 undergraduate men questioned in a study conducted by Charlene L. Muehlenhard of Texas A&M University and Richard M. McFall of Indiana University, almost all felt it was fine for the woman to make the first move. Provided the man liked her, he would accept the invitation. Muehlenhard gave her subjects three descriptions of dates which varied in respect to who initiated it, where the couple went, and who paid. Results showed that men rated intercourse against the woman's wishes as significantly more justifiable when: (1) the woman initiated the date; (2) the couple went to the man's apartment rather than to the movies or a religious function; and (3) when the man paid the expenses for the evening. It appears, then, that a woman's assertive actions may be interpreted by men as justification for rape.

There is no real protection against acquaintance rape, no way of knowing that a friendly invitation for dinner will lead to something more or that the "nice" man who takes his date home will decide he wants sex and will get it, even if it means violence to some degree. The best prevention techniques are awareness, assertiveness, learning common-sense avoidance strategies to diffuse potential situations and, perhaps, fighting for rights. The use of alcohol and drugs is often related to incidents of acquaintance rape: when people are intoxicated or "high," they may act in atypical ways.

In 1979 Groth and Birnbaum reported a three-stage pattern in rapists' behavior concerning acquaintance rapes. First, a rapist will invade a woman's personal space (for instance, by putting his hand on a woman's knee in a public place). If the victim does not object, the rapist will escalate the intrusive behavior. Third, the rapist will get the victim in an isolated place and attack.

Those who do not feel good about themselves are vulnerable to exploitation by others. People develop positive or negative self-esteem based on reflections of how others see them. If we are repeatedly told that we are worthless, we will not feel that we have the right to ask others for things we want. Also, it is difficult to reject peer group standards if we believe that the only way to be a valuable person is to associate with others who are valuable. Take, for example, the case of a young woman with low self-esteem who dates the captain of a football team in order to raise her own value. If he tells her that he will not continue going out with her unless she has sex with him, she may comply to maintain her status as his "girlfriend." He may also tell her that "everyone else is having sex, and something is wrong with people who don't." She may feel that he really knows much more about sex than she does and so may be willing to have sex with him — even though she does *not* think it is what *she* wants to do.

Acquaintance rape is rape nonetheless and, as such, it is a crime of violence, motivated by the desire to control and dominate, and not by sex. Whenever a woman is forced to have sex, even if the man knows the woman — and even if he has had sex with her before — rape is being committed.

In order to minimize the likelihood of date rape, women must assert themselves and stay in control of their environment. Watching for non-verbal cues and staying clear of vulnerable settings are practical precautions. Also, although women have been taught and encouraged to "play the dating game," they should realize that passivity, submissiveness, and coyness are themselves dangerous and can create a climate for sexual aggression.

If both partners on a date *really* communicate what they mean and listen to the needs of the other person, some of the problems leading to acquaintance rape can be eliminated. Treat each other as equals, and believe that you two really are. Respect your partner, and enjoy your date. □

Dr. Andrea Parrot is a professor of human sexuality at Cornell University in Ithaca, New York.

Acquaintance Rape:

Between Men and Women

by, Roz Kenworthy, Sex Counselor and Janis Talbot, Health Educator

—A Cornell co-ed goes to a party with three of her women friends. She meets a man and spends the entire evening dancing and talking with him. Her friends want to go home and decide to leave without her since she seems to be having a good time. Later that evening, reluctant to walk home alone, she accepts the man's offer to stay in his room for the night. They have intercourse against her will. She has been raped.

—A man and a woman have been romantically involved with each other for months. The woman does not want to have intercourse; she just wants to be held and kissed. The man doesn't stop his kissing and fondling; he forces her to have intercourse despite her persistent pleas to stop. She has been raped.

—A woman has been admiring a man in one of her classes and asks him out on a date. The man accepts and they go out for a few drinks. On the way home the man drives her to his apartment for a cup of coffee. At his apartment he forces her to have intercourse with him. She has been raped.

Each of these fictional situations suggests circumstance in which acquaintance rape occurs at Cornell. A woman who is psychologically or physically pressured into sexual intercourse, against her will, by someone she knows or has reason to trust is a victim of acquaintance rape. We are considering here neither the legalities involved nor the phenomenon of violent rape by strangers. In most cases of rape on this campus, the rapist is known to and trusted by the victim. Victims are most often women, although men are occasionally assaulted sexually. Some of the social concerns both men and women have about the problem of acquaintance rape will be considered here, as well as strategies that can be used to prevent such incidents. We hope this discussion will lead to awareness of the problem and further consideration of ways that individuals and groups can help to eliminate the occurrence of acquaintance rape.

with Andrea Parrot, Lecturer in Human Service Studies Department

In the first situation described, let's call the woman Jennifer and the man Tom. Jennifer has always taken it for granted that it is highly desirable for a woman to be attractive to a man. The alternative would be to grow up like Aunt Sally, always the butt of family jokes about how she was too tall and awkward and strong for any man to look twice at her. Jennifer, on this particular evening, is excited about the attention she has been getting from Tom. He's the first appealing man she has meet at Cornell; he's fascinating to talk to and a wonderful dancer. She's having such a good time she's hardly noticing how much she's had to drink or how tired she is. When Tom offers to let her sleep in his room instead of going home in the rain, it makes her think he may be interested in her, too. It's really nice of him to offer his bed when it means he'll have to sleep on the floor.

But what is likely to be going on in Tom's mind? He is really pleased to have run across a good-looking woman who is so responsive to him. When she agrees to spend the night with him, he's delighted that she isn't one of those stubborn women who insists on a deep relationship before she'll let him touch her. When she realizes what is happening and insists that she does not want to have intercourse, he doesn't believe her. As soon as he "comes," he falls asleep and is completely unaware of her getting dressed and leaving his room with tears streaming down her face. When he calls her the next day, he is amazed that she hangs up as soon as she hears his voice. Later, he is flabbergasted when a Safety Division officer appears at his door to discuss the rape of a co-ed the night before.

How could this acquaintance rape have been avoided? Both Jennifer and Tom might have asked themselves whether they were making unfounded assumptions. Tom was taking it for granted that any woman as friendly and as sensitive as Jennifer would know that a man

Reprinted by the permission of the publisher from *Vital Signs* (Cornell University Health Services), Vol. 4, No. 1, September 1984.

couldn't spend a whole evening dancing and messing around without expecting to have intercourse. She wouldn't agree to spend the night otherwise. Tom thinks women say "no" even when they mean "yes," and he believes that women play hard to get. It made him feel powerful to have sex with Jennifer over her feeble objections.

Jennifer, on the other hand, was caught up in her own view of what was happening, unable to perceive the realities of the present because of her hopes for the future. She hardly noticed when her friends left the party; it never occurred to her that she was taking a chance by spending the night with Tom. She assumed he would know that her responsiveness meant that she was really interested in a relationship with him. Nothing could have been further from her mind than the idea that a future boyfriend would take advantage of her sexually. She didn't dream that the problem of establishing limits would ever arise.

The prevention of acquaintance rape starts with a careful examination of your assumptions about yourself and about the other person. *Women may benefit by asking themselves:*

1. How much physical contact do I want during this encounter?

2. Am I letting him know, specifically and unambiguously, what I want both physically and emotionally? Is my non-verbal behavior suggesting that I want physical intimacy?

3. Am I able to say no? Can I say it clearly and assertively?

4. Can I control myself and this situation so that I have what I want and avoid what I don't want? Have either of us had too much to drink or too much of any other drug? Are my judgements fuzzy?

5. Can I leave if I want to? Is the door locked? Do I have the keys to my/his car? Is it safe for me to walk home? Can I run in the shoes I'm wearing? Will anyone hear me and be likely to respond if I shout?

Questions for men:

1. Am I putting my own needs and expectations ahead of hers?

2. Am I assuming that she feels the same as I do about having intercourse at this time? Have I asked her what she wants? Have I been listening to what she says—even if it's different from what I want?

3. Am I assuming that when a woman says "no" she means "yes?"

4. Why do I want to have intercourse with her? Is it to satisfy my ego? Will it make me feel powerful? Is this the only way I can express caring and interest?

5. How will I feel about this tomorrow if she says she never wanted to have intercourse?

6. Do I want to have intercourse with someone who isn't sure she wants to have it with me or is unclear about it?

Questions for a couple:

1. Are we really communicating—in detail—about our emotional/physical needs and expectations?

2. Are we clearly stating what we want and expect? Are we failing to express thoughts or feelings we're afraid the other person might reject?

3. Are our verbal and non-verbal cues consistent? Are our bodies saying one thing and our minds saying another?

4. Are we protected against unwanted pregnancy and against sexually transmitted diseases?

Couples need to formulate additional questions to deal adequately with their specific situations. For example, in the second scene described above, the man may need to ask himself, "Am I confusing love with sex? Am I assuming she doesn't really love me unless she gives in to intercourse?"

Honest, careful consideration of all such questions will only help when men and women deeply want to avoid serious misunderstanding. In cases where a man is determined to demonstrate his strength and superior power, at any cost, and he chooses a woman as the vehicle for his demonstration, violent rape is the result. Then, sadly, attempts at communication of the kind we are recommending are irrelevant. However, such cases are pertinent to this discussion in several ways:

— Sexual desire is incidental in rape.

— All rape centers in the rapist's conscious or unconscious desire to control and dominate the victim.

— All rape involves disregard of the victim's need to control her body and her personal environment.

— All rape is wrong.

Why Nice Men Force Sex on Their Friends:

The Problem of Acquaintance Rape

The typical image of a rapist is a crazed maniac who jumps out of the bushes, brandishes a knife or gun, and forces a woman to have sex with him. Images like this are strong and lasting, but they mask the essential fact that most rapes are committed by acquaintances and lovers. The false image lives on because few rapes by acquaintances are reported; in fact, those involved often do not recognize that a rape has occurred.

The legal definition of rape is a victim having sexual intercourse against her will and without her consent (Burkhart, 1983). Sexual assault is defined as a sexual encounter other than intercourse (such as oral and anal sex) against the victim's will and without his or her consent. In many states only a woman can be legally raped by a man, but the FBI estimates that 10 percent of all sexual assault victims are men. The victim does not have to be threatened with a danger-ous weapon or be injured for an inci-dent to be considered rape. Coercion or threat of force or violence are suffi-cient (FBI, 1982).

Socializing factors

How can "nice" men with "good inten-tions" coerce someone to have sex? It is because men and women, in the pro-cess of becoming social beings, learn communication patterns that make acquaintance rape likely.

In our culture, men are taught to view women as either virtuous or sexually loose, which contributes to uncertainty about female desires. Men are taught to not take women seri-ously, that women do not really mean what they say. Young women are taught that males know more about sex than females, so the female should comply with the male's demand. Both males and females feel that certain

behavior allows a man to force sex, such as the woman "leading the man on."

These uncertainties are often based on the reluctance of women and men to express their feelings. Many times in verbal communication, if something is clearly wrong with a woman (she is crying or slamming doors) and she is asked what is wrong, she may say "nothing," rather than express her true feelings. Men display this same type of behavior, expressing anger or frustra-tion by punching walls, or speaking through clenched teeth, but still saying nothing is wrong. The message is that in a situation where verbal and non-verbal messages are inconsistent, the verbal message is not accurate.

In sexual situations the verbal and nonverbal messages are frequently inconsistent. This inconsistency was often established when a boy was told by his mother, his teacher (usually female), or another woman in a posi-tion of authority to do something. If he didn't the consequences would be severe. If the deadline was then extended or the consequence was not severe, he learned that those women did not mean what they said.

Some men do not believe a woman's verbal messages in sexual encounters either. In fact, a man may actually feel he is doing a woman a favor by pushing her sexually; if she says no to a sexual overture, she may really want to say yes but is afraid she will be viewed as loose. He thinks she says no because she is worried about her reputation, not because she really does not want to have sex with him. So if he pushes her, even if she is

---

Andrea Parrot

Andrea Parrot is a lecturer in human service studies in the College of Human Ecology.

saying no, they will both ultimately get what they want: she will get sex without tarnishing her reputation, and he will be satisfied. In this type of interaction the male feels that he is acting as he should and would prob-ably be surprised to find that some women really mean it when they say no.

Women and men also believe that men should know more about sex. If he tells her that "everyone else is having sex" and that "something is wrong with people who don't," she may be willing to have sex with him, even though it is not what she wants to do.

There is also tremendous peer pres-sure for the male to have sex on a date. Even if he does not want to initiate sex, a man may feel he has to or his date will think he is gay. He is encouraged by other young men to "score" sexually to be considered manly. The woman, even if she does not want sex, may think that the man finds her unattractive if he does not initiate sex. These pressures are responsible for people having sex when neither want it.

It is difficult to reject group stan-dards if one believes that the only way to be a valuable person is to be asso-ciated with others who are valuable. A young woman who has low self-esteem may date the captain of the football team in order to raise her value. If the male in this situation uses coercion by telling her he will not continue going out with her unless she has sex with him, she may comply to maintain her status as his girlfriend.

When forced sex becomes "accept-able"

Some men feel that a particular female behavior permits a man to force a woman to have sex. Charlene L.

Mulenhard of Texas A&M University and Richard McFall of Indiana University reported the results of a study in which 106 college students were asked to respond anonymously about acceptable behavior in dating situations.

The subjects were given descriptions of three types of dates that varied in respect to who initiated the date, where the couple went, and who paid. They were then asked if there were any circumstances in which forced sex was justified. Men rated intercourse against the woman's wishes as significantly more justifiable when the woman initiated the date, when the man paid, and when the couple went to the man's apartment (Mulenhard and McFall 1981).

UCLA researchers posed similar questions to teens. A high percentage of the male teens felt that forced sex was acceptable if the woman said yes and then changed her mind (54 percent), if he spent a lot of money on her (39 percent), if she "led him on" (54 percent), and if he is so turned on that he thinks he can't stop (36 percent) (Giarrusso, et al. 1979).

Patterns in acquaintance rape

Groth and Birnbaum (1979) reported a three-stage pattern in rapists' behavior concerning acquaintance rapes. First, a rapist will invade a woman's personal space (for instance, by putting his hand on a woman's knee in a public place). This is common in fraternity parties and in bars when the music is so loud the couple must be close to hear each other.

If the woman does not object, the rapist proceeds to the second stage in which he will desensitize her to the intrusion by escalating the behavior (moving his hand to her buttocks, for example). It is unlikely that she would tell him that she was uncomfortable

with his "roaming hands," but she may feel uneasy as a result of this behavior and suggest going someplace less crowded. She does not want her friends to see how forward he is being, and she does not want to stay close to him. He may misinterpret her suggestion as her way to be alone with him. The third stage is when they are in an isolated place and the rapist attacks.

This is a general pattern in acquaintance rape, and though all victims and rapists are different, alcohol and drugs are often involved in incidents of acquaintance rape. In a study of rape in Canada, alcohol was used by half of all offenders and by one-third of the victims (British Columbia Rape Prevention Project 1980). This is important for young adults, since peer group expectations usually include consumption of alcohol at social events.

Solution to the problem

There are many things men can do to view forced sex for what it is, and to begin to try to stop it on a personal or societal level. First, they must understand that forced or coercive sex is rape, even if the women are friends or lovers. It is never acceptable to force yourself on a woman, even if you think she's been teasing and leading you on or you have heard that women say no but mean yes. It is not "manly" to use force to get your way.

Women should be aware that their assertive actions may be interpreted by men as justification for rape. This does not mean that women should avoid using assertive behavior with men, but that they be aware of how assertiveness may be interpreted by men.

Since socialization is responsible for many sex attitudes, both men and women must be willing to explore the importance of traditional socialization on their behavior. College men, for

example, are exerting peer pressure to condemn, rather than condone, the notion of women as conquests. Adult females who influence male children must be clear about messages, truthful about feelings, and consistent in disciplining. Failure to do so may lead to young men not taking women's verbal messages seriously.

Once these men become adults themselves they have the potential to influence the socialization of children. They can teach children about the importance of viewing women as equals, and the importance of communicating their feelings clearly and consistently.

References

British Columbia Rape Prevention Project. *Rape Prevention Resource Manual,* based on a study of rape in Canada and Vancouver. MTI Teleprograms, 1980.

Burkhart, B. "Acquaintance Rape Statistics and Prevention." A paper presented at the Acquaintance Rape and Rape Prevention on Campus Conference in Louisville, Kentucky, December, 1983.

FBI. *Uniform Crime Reports,* Washington D.C.: U.S. Government Printing Office, 1982.

Giarrusso, R., Johnson, P., Goodchilds, J., and Zellman, G. "Adolescent Cues and Signals: Sex and Sexual Assault." A paper presented to a symposium of the Western Psychological Association Meeting, April 1979, San Diego, Calif.

Groth, A. N. *Men Who Rape: The Psychology of the Offender.* New York: Plenum, 1979.

Mulenhard, C. L., and R. M. McFall. "Dating Initiation from a Woman's Perspective." *Behavior Therapy.* 12 (1981).

Appendix V

UNDERSTANDING THE LAW

Forcing or coercing someone to have sexual intercourse or engage in other sexual contact is against the law. Specifically, in New York State if a woman is forced to have sexual intercourse or if she is unable to consent, the behavior of the perpetrator is considered rape. The force necessary can be any amount or threat of physical force which places the woman in fear of injury or in fear for her life. The perpetrator does not need to use a weapon or beat her to make her fearful of injury or for her life.

She is considered unable to consent if she is mentally incapacitated or is physically helpless due to drug or alcohol consumption, is mentally defective, is asleep, or is less than 17 years of age. If a female has intercourse under these circumstances, it is rape.

Forcing or coercing a man or woman to engage in any sexual contact other than sexual intercourse under the circumstances mentioned above is considered sexual abuse or sodomy.

Members of the Cornell community who commit these crimes will be subject to harsh sanctions from the University and/or the criminal justice system including but not limited to:

Prosecution through the Judicial Administrator's office which could result in:

- probation

- suspension

- expulsion

- termination of employment

- financial restitution

- and/or other sanctions

Prosecution in the criminal courts (felony or misdemeanor)

Prosecution in the civil court

Fraternity sanctions

- probation

- rescinding recognition

The Cornell community condemns sexual abuse and acquaintance or stranger rape; these actions constitute violation of the Campus Code of Conduct as well as New York State Law. Cornell University provides counseling and other supportive services in cases of sexual abuse and acquaintance or stranger rape. Confidential inquiries may by made at the following offices:

On Campus

- Judicial Administrator – 255-4680

- Public Safety – 255-1111

- Dean of Students – 255-6858

- COSEP – 255-3841

- International Students Office – 255-5243

- Lesbian & Gay Peer Counseling – 255-6482

- Gannett Health Center

- Contraception, Gynecology, Sexuality Service (CGSS) – 255-3978

■ Sex Counselor – 255-6448

■ Psychological Service, Ground Floor – 255-5208

■ Overnight Unit – 255-5155

■ Cornell United Religious Work – 255-4214

■ Empathy, Assistance and Referral Service: EARS – 255-3277

■ Residence Life Staff – 255-5511

Off Campus

■ Ithaca Rape Crisis Center – 272-1616

■ Planned Parenthood – 273-1513

■ Task Force for Battered Women – 272-1616

■ Suicide Prevention and Crisis Service of Ithaca – 272-1616

■ For further information contact the Dean of Students Office – 255-6858

Note: You must revise this to reflect your state law, campus policies and local resources.

PART IIII

SELECTED ARTICLES

Date Rape

Andrea Parrot, PhD

You can help the victim to regain a sense of control over her life, improve self-esteem, and avoid future acquaintance rapes.

As many as 15%–25% of college age women have been sexually assaulted or raped by an acquaintance, recent studies show.[1,2] An even higher rate probably occurs in the general population, and marital rape occurs as well.[3,4] Not all acquaintance rape victims are female: The FBI estimates that 10% of all sexual assault victims are male. (The pronoun "she" will be used in this article to refer to victims of date rape since most are female.) Men rarely report this crime unless they are physically injured. In fact, most date rape victims do not report the crime to the police or any other authority since they may not define their experience as rape or may feel partly responsible and therefore guilty.

Most date rape victims believe the myth that a sexual attack is a rape *only* when a stranger violently attacks a woman and injures or kills her while she is fighting him off. In fact, rape is what happens anytime a victim is forced to have sex (usually vaginal intercourse) against her will. Moreover, if sex takes place when the woman is unconscious, or if she is under the age of consent or is physically or mentally incapacitated, the act meets the legal definition of rape in most jurisdictions. Similarly, rape occurs if the victim capitulates to sex out of fear for his or her physical safety.

Identifying the victim

The date rape victim who believes her action or behavior "caused" the rape may tell you only that she "got into a bad situation." She may feel guilty and responsible for the rape and therefore probably will not report it. Instead, it'll be your task to determine whether the patient has indeed been raped. You can do this by taking a particularly careful history and looking for symptoms of the rape trauma syndrome (Table).[5,6] Since it is such a common occurrence, it is advisable to discuss date rape with every adolescent patient during an office vis-

it, since date rape occurs most often between the ages of 15 and 25 years.

What to ask. Getting the truth out of the patient may be difficult. The following questions will help:

• Have you ever had sex when you didn't want to?

• Have you ever been forced to have sex?

• Do you have difficulty saying "no" when you don't want to have sex?

What not to ask. Don't discredit the victim by subtly placing unfair blame on her. Avoid questions such as:

• Have you had sex with this person before?

• Are you married to the man who forced you to have sex?

• Did you fight back or sustain any injuries during the unwanted sexual encounter?

• Were you drunk at the time?

Preventive teaching for adolescent boys/men. All patients, male as well as female, need relevant medical and legal information about rape. Adolescent boys need this information especially urgently, since they may commit date/acquaintance rape without thinking they are do-

Andrea Parrot is Assistant Professor, Department of Human Service Studies, Cornell University, Ithaca, NY.

Reprinted by permission of the publisher from *Medical Aspects of Human Sexuality*, April 1990.

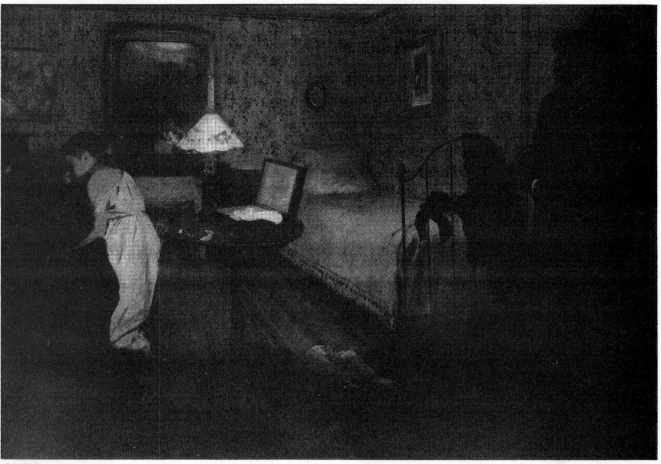

"Interior"
by Edgar Degas (1834–1917)

ing anything wrong. Many grow up believing that a woman's "no" never really means "no" and that if the man persists, he will get what he wants.

Effects of date rape

Three typical behavior patterns may be observed in acquaintance rape victims, either immediately after the rape or years afterwards, according to one researcher[7]:

• Withdrawal from social interactions. The victim does not feel she can trust her own judgment, because she once chose to date a rapist. Therefore, she stops making any decisions requiring judg-

ment and withdraws from social interactions.

• Repression of the rape memory. In the attempt to get back to normal, the victim may repress her memory of the rape; once under stress and reminded of the rape, however, she may explode emotionally. Such a reaction may be triggered by an act as simple as being touched on the shoulder by a man or being examined by a male gynecologist. This reaction to reminders of the rape may precipitate recurring crises.

• Nondiscriminatory sexual behavior. If the victim was a virgin before the rape, she may conclude

that she is now "a bad person" and has no legitimate reason to refuse any requests for sex. She may therefore adopt a sexually promiscuous behavior pattern.

If the victim shows any of these behavior patterns, she needs counseling that will help her to overcome feelings of guilt and self-blame. Such feelings often play havoc with the woman's interpersonal relationships and her self-esteem.

The physician's role

Believe the victim. If you counsel a patient who is a date rape victim, start by believing her.

Table. Rape trauma syndrome[5,6]	
Acute phase (may last for several weeks)	
Expressive reactions 　Angry 　Fearful 　Anxious 　Tense	Controlled reaction 　Composed 　Calm 　Subdued
Long-term reorganization phase (may last for years)	
Sleep disturbances Exaggerated startle response Guilt Impaired memory or power of concentration Avoidance of others and social situations Mistrust of men Defensiveness, both physical and emotional Rapid mood swings Self-blame Headaches Feeling that she is "going crazy"	

Such patients stand to gain little from lying and in fact may lose the support and friendship of family and friends by reporting an acquaintance rape. This is particularly true if the family and friends know the assailant and feel forced to choose whom to believe: him or the victim. Indeed, the false report rate for date rape is very low.[8] Emotionally healthy people do not falsely accuse others of crimes. Thus, if a patient reports what turns out to be an imaginary rape, she needs a psychiatric referral.

Refer for counseling. You can help the rape-traumatized woman regain a sense of control over her life, improve self-esteem, and avoid future acquaintance/date rapes by referring her to specially trained counselors at a local rape crisis center. Caution: Counselors trained to help victims raped by a *stranger* may do more harm than good if they have not been taught how to counsel *acquaintance rape* victims. Regardless of what led to the date rape— even if the woman went to the apartment of a man she did not know very well—she should never be blamed for having caused the rape to occur.

Let the victim choose the best options. Your patient can overcome her rape experience by taking some of the following actions:

• Tell her family.
• Tell her friends.
• Seek therapy.
• Confront her assailant.
• Report the rape to the police.
• Press criminal charges.
• Sue the assailant in civil court.
• Report the rape to school authorities.

Your patient may want to confront the assailant after the event (when she is feeling stronger) to tell him her reactions to what he did to her. (She may prefer to do this in a safe, public place and with a support person present.) She can give information to the police without being obliged to give her name or press charges, or she can press criminal charges against her assailant. She may also sue him in civil court for pain and suffering and for the recovery of therapy costs. She may, in fact, have a better chance of winning in civil than in criminal court.

If the rapist is a student, the victim can report the rape to the school authorities. If both victim and assailant attend the same institution, the rapist may be transferred, suspended, or expelled so she will not have to see him every day in her classes.

Teach avoidance tactics. Regardless of what the victim decides to do about reporting the assault or seeking help, she needs to learn how to become less vulnerable so that she can avoid situations likely to end in date rape in the future. She must learn to assess potentially dangerous situations and exercise assertive behavior to get out of them or avoid them completely. For instance, she can learn to use her voice as a weapon by yelling or saying when threatened, "Stop it. This is rape." She can also defend herself verbally against a date who tries to exploit her.

To succeed, she must have enough self-esteem to believe in her right to defend herself against someone she knows and likes but who is trying to force her to do something against her will. However, even if she does not defend herself by any of these means and is raped, she is not to blame. The rapist is the one who is guilty of the crime, not the victim.

Conclusion

The most important thing a victim can do to regain control over her life is to place blame and responsibility for the rape where it belongs—with the rapist. Since date rape is usually nonviolent, the woman is not likely to have any physical evidence of trauma. The psychological trauma of rape, however, may lead to other symptoms such as depression, eating disorders, or acting out sexually (a response requiring medical intervention). You can best aid your patient's recovery when you promptly identify the woman who has been raped, treat her physical symptoms, help her determine a course of action, and refer her to a specially trained counselor. If the woman is involved in a sexual relationship, it may be advisable for both partners to enter counseling jointly.   ♂♀

References

1. Koss M, Gidycz C: Sexual experiences survey: Reliability and validity. *J Consult Clin Psychol* 53(3):422, 1985.
2. Parrot A: Comparison of acquaintance rape patterns among college students in a large co-ed university and a small women's college. Read before the 1985 National Society for the Scientific Study of Sex Convention. November 1985, San Diego.
3. Koss MP, Gidycz CA, Wisinewski N: The scope of rape: Incidence and prevalence of sexual aggression and victimization in a national sample of higher education students. *J Consult Clin Psychol* 55(2):162, 1987.
4. Russell DEH: The prevalence and incidence of rape and attempted rape of females. *Victimology* 7:81, 1982.
5. Burgess AW, Holstrom LL: Rape trauma syndrome. *Am J Psychiatry* 131:981, 1974.
6. Nadelson C, Nortman M, Zackson H, et al: A follow-up study of rape victims. *Am J Psychiatry* 139:1226, 1982.
7. Burkhart B: Acquaintance rape statistics and prevention. Read before the Acquaintance Rape and Prevention on Campus Conference. December 1983, Louisville, KY.
8. Warshaw R: *I Never Called It Rape*. New York, Harper and Row, 1988.

Adolescents' Attitudes about Acquaintance Rape

Andrea Parrot

Kim, a high school junior, has dated several members of the football team. She has a reputation for being "easy" among its members. On her first date with Erik, the team's quarterback, they went to a party at the house of a friend, whose parents were out of town for the weekend. They were enjoying getting to know each other, drinking beer, dancing, and kissing on the dance floor during slow songs. Erik loved to watch Kim because she was such a seductive dancer. Toward the end of the evening, after they had both had quite a bit to drink, Kim suggested that they go somewhere so they could be alone to "talk." Erik agreed, and drove them to a quiet, secluded park. He turned the car off, and they started making out. Kim responded positively to Erik's sexual advances until he started to take her pants off. She said "no," but he told her that he knew she really wanted it, and besides he knew she liked to "do it." Kim was hoping Erik would stop, and she kept telling him "no," but he just kept telling her to "relax and enjoy it." Erik was on top of her in the back seat of the car. Erik didn't notice that tears were running down Kim's cheeks when he penetrated her. After Erik ejaculated he gave Kim a tender kiss on her forehead, told her how much he enjoyed it, got dressed, and drove her home. He called her several days later to see if she was free to go out with him again the next weekend.

Most teenagers would not call what happened between Kim and Erik a rape, although legally and morally it is rape. Many teenagers think that forced sex is acceptable under many different circumstances, that there is a point beyond which a women gives up the right to say no, and that in sex no doesn't really mean no (Goodchilds et al. 1988; Kikuchi 1988; Goodchilds and Zellman 1984). Some male and female teens subscribe to these views, but generally males are likely to believe them more often. Sexual assault and rape on dates happens often, and is experienced by approximately 20 percent of college women in the United States (Koss, Gidycz, and Wisniewski 1987).

When Los Angeles high school students were studied regarding acceptability of forced sex, more than half of the males felt that it was acceptable for a male to force sex if the female first said yes even if she later changed her mind (Giarruso et al. 1979). It is possible that the female was saying yes to kissing, not to intercourse. If she is not specific about what she is saying yes to, he may interpret the yes to imply that sexual intercourse is what she wants (Parrot 1987).

More than a third of the males in the Los Angeles study believed that forced sex was acceptable if the male spent "a lot" of money on the female, or if he is so "turned on" that he thinks he cannot stop. Almost a third of the female subjects felt that forced sex was acceptable if the couple had dated a long time, if she says that she is going to have sex with him and then changes her mind, if she lets him touch her above the waist, and if she "led him on" (Giarrusso et al. 1979).

Male adolescents in that study indicated more cues as indicative of willingness to have

Reprinted by permission of the publisher from the *Human Ecology Forum*, Winter 1990.

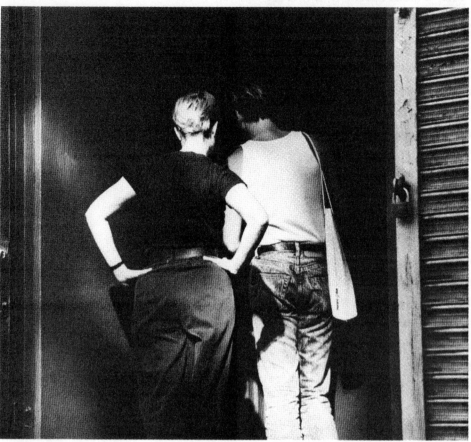

DEDE HATCH

sex than did females: revealing clothing worn by either person; male's prior reputation; date locations such as at his home or at the beach at night; drinking alcohol together; and paying a compliment to a date. Females were less likely to think these were cues for sex (Goodchilds and Zellman 1984). When those teens were asked if a woman ever gives up her right to say "no," three-fourths of the males and over half of the females believed that forced sex was acceptable in some circumstances (Goodchilds et al. 1988).

When Rhode Island teenagers were asked if forced sex is ever justified, half felt that a female was asking to be raped if she walked alone at night and dressed seductively and that a female's "bad" sexual reputation can justify forced sex

(Kikuchi 1988). A quarter of the males and 6 percent of the females said that a man had a right to force sex on a date if he spent money on her. Two-thirds of the males and half of the females believed that forced sex was acceptable if the couple had been dating for more than six months (Kikuchi 1988).

Adolescents learn "sexual scripts," which establish the social norms that say the male should be the initiator and the female should be the "limit setter" (La-Plante, McCormick, and Brannigan 1980). Male sexual aggression is viewed by young people as an inevitable part of the date game (Berger et al. 1986). Adolescents also believe that young women are responsible for controlling how far sex will go on a date, and if the female cannot control her partner it is her own

fault (Berger et al. 1986). Young men are socialized to believe that if a female says no she really means yes, and if she agrees to any sexual activity she is also agreeing to having sexual intercourse (Dull and Giacopassi 1987). Therefore, misunderstanding and misperception of sexual cues are the norm in dating situations (Burkhart and Stanton 1988).

When people subscribe to these views about sex and relationships they consider forced sex acceptable under certain circumstances, and they are likely to excuse rape. Women who hold these beliefs are more likely to be vulnerable to victimization, and if they are raped, they will probably blame themselves and not report the rape. If victims do not report the event or seek help, their emotional recovery will be very slow.

Attitude change is necessary to decrease acquaintance rapes. Unfortunately, attitude change is very difficult because teenagers have been exposed to rape supportive beliefs since early childhood. Family, schools, media, and peers all contribute to young peoples' attitudes about acceptable sexual behaviors, which may contribute to acquaintance rape (Parrot 1989).

Continuum of adolescent sexual behaviors

Adolescents' sexual behavior often begins with mutual sexual exploration, but may also include other behaviors that fall along a continuum, which at one extreme could be considered forced sex. The differences between behaviors on the continuum may be so subtle that those involved may not be able to differentiate clearly between acceptable and unacceptable behaviors.

Bateman and Stringer (1984) have proposed several stages in adolescent sexual behavior, as shown in the figure below. *Mutual sexual exploration* (initiating sexual activity, touching and mutual

Figure 1. Teenage Sexual Experiences Continuum (*Adapted from Bateman and Stringer, 1984.*)

1	**2**	**3**	**4**	**5**	**6**
Mutual Sexual Exploration	Persuasion of a reluctant partner	Exploitative activity	Sexual coercion	Sexual harassment	Acquaintance rape

pleasure giving) is a normal part of adolescent psycho-sexual development. That stage shares some elements with *persuasion* of a reluctant partner. When persuasion is used, both parties may feel good about the encounter if the reluctant partner is treated with respect and his or her feelings are taken into account. The next stage on the continuum is *exploitative* sexual activity, which may involve the same behaviors as persuasion; however, the reluctant partner's wishes and feelings are not taken into account. In exploitative sexual activity the reluctant partner is coerced or threatened to comply. One partner may *sexually harass* the other by violating the victim in a sexual manner. *Acquaintance rape* may follow harassment behavior if one partner is forced to have sex by the other partner. (Date rape is considered one form of acquaintance rape.)

The difference between these stages on the continuum are often subtle, and may not be clear to adolescents, especially if those involved are under the influence of drugs or alcohol.

Rewriting the script
Attitudes that contribute to acquaintance rape are common among adolescents. Adolescents generally believe that males have stronger sex drives than females, and once sexually aroused, men have difficulty controlling themselves (Goodchilds et al. 1984; Jackson 1978). This belief, combined with the male role as initiator in sexual interactions, contributes to males feeling justified in forcing sexual intercourse on an unwilling sexual partner (White and Humphrey, in press).

Unfortunately, rape-prone attitudes sometimes do contribute to acquaintance rape among adolescents. These attitudes can be changed by providing more responsible messages and accurate information in the media. Parents also need to instill ethical values in their children that indicate it is not acceptable for one person to exploit another. Schools have also been successful in changing young people's attitudes about acquaintance rape. Acquaintance rape is a serious problem affecting teenagers as well as adults. We may begin to decrease the number of acquaintance rapes by chang-

ing the way we socialize adolescents about acceptable sexual attitudes and behaviors.

References
White, Jacquelyn, and J. Humphrey (in press). "Young People's Attitudes about Acquaintance Rape." In A. Parrot, and L. Bechhofer (eds.). *Hidden Rape: Sexual Assault among Acquaintances, Friends, and Intimates.* New York: Wiley and Sons.

Bateman, P., and G. Stringer. 1984. *Where Do I Start? A Parent's Guide to Talking to Teens about Acquaintance Rape.* Teen Acquaintance Rape: A Community Response Project. Seattle, Wash.

Berger, R.J., P. Searles, R.G. Salem, and B. A. Pierce.1986. "Sexual Assault in a College Community." *Sociological Focus* 19:1-26.

Burkhart, B.R.,and A. L. Stanton. 1988. "Sexual Aggression in Acquaintance Rape Relationships." In G.W. Russell (ed.), *Violence in Intimate Relationships.* New York: PMA Publishing.

Dull, R.T. , and D. J. Giacopassi. 1987. "Demographic Correlates of Sexual and Dating Attitudes." *Criminal Justice and Behavior* 14:175-93.

Giarrusso, R., P. Johnson, J. Goodchilds, and G. Zellman, G. 1979. "Adolescent Cues and Signals: Sexual Assault." Paper presented to a symposium of the Western Psychological Association Meeting, San Diego, Calif.

Goodchilds, J.D., and G. L. Zellman. 1984. "Sexual Signaling and Sexual Aggression in Adolescent Relationships." In N.M. Malmuth and E. Donnerstein (eds.) *Pornography and Sexual Aggression.*

Orlando, Fla: Academic Press, 233-43.

Goodchilds, J.D., G. Zellman, P. Johnson, and R. Giarrusso.1988. "Adolescents and Their Perceptions of Sexual Interactions." In A.W. Burgess (ed.), *Rape and Sexual Assault,*Vol. II. New York: Garland.

Jackson, S. 1978. "The Social Context of Rape: Sexual Scripts and Motivation." *Women's Studies International Quarterly* 1: 27-38.

Kikuchi, J.J. 1988. "What Do Adolescents Know and Think about Sexual Abuse?" A paper presented at the National Symposium on Child Victimization, Anaheim, CA.

Koss, M.P.,C. A. Gidycz, and N. Wisniewski. 1987. "The Scope of Rape: Incidence and Prevalence of Sexual Aggression and Victimization in a National Sample of Higher Education Students." *Journal of Consulting And Clinical Psychology* 34: 186-96.

LaPlante, M.N., N. McCormick, and G. G. Brannigan. 1980. "Living the Sexual Scripts: College Students' Views of Influence in Sexual Encounters." *The Journal of Sex Research* 16: 338-55.

Parrot, A. 1989. "Acquaintance Rape among Adolescents: Identifying Risk Groups and Intervention Strategies." *Journal of Social Work and Human Sexuality.* 8 (1): 47-60.

Parrot, A. 1987. *Facilitator's Manual for STOP DATE RAPE!* Ithaca, New York: Cornell University.

Andrea Parrot

Andrea Parrot is an assistant professor in the Department of Human Service Studies, where she teaches about health services, including a course on human sexuality that draws up to 1,000 students a year. Her research is on acquaintance rape, and she consults, testifies, and lectures frequently on sexuality topics. She is author of *Coping with Date Rape and Acquaintance Rape* (Rosen), co-editor with Harold Feldman of *Human Sexuality: Contemporary Controversies,* and co-editor with L. Bechhofer of *Hidden Rape: Sexual Assault between Acquaintances, Friends, and Intimates* (Wiley).

PART IV

RAPE AND SEXUAL
ASSAULT BIBLIOGRAPHIES

BOOKS AND MONOGRAPHS

Adams, C., and Fay, J. (1984). *Nobody told me that it was rape.* Santa Cruz: Net work Publications.

Adams, D.; Fay, J.; and Loreen-Martin, J. (1984). *No is not enough: Helping teenagers avoid sexual assault.* San Luis Obispo, CA: Impact Publishers.

Ageton, S.S. (1983). *Sexual assault among adolescents.* Lexington, MA: D.C. Heath and Company.

Amir, M. (1971). *Patterns in forcible rape.* Chicago: University of Chicago Press.

Bart, P.B., and O'Brien, P.H. (1985). *Stopping rape: Successful survival strategies.* New York: Pergamon Press.

Benedict, H. (1985). *Recovery - How to survive sexual assault for women, men, teenagers, their friends and families.* Garden City, NY: Doubleday & Company, Inc.

Beneke, T. (1982). *Men on rape: What they have to say about sexual violence.* New York: St. Martin's Press.

Bourque, L.B. (1989). Defining rape. Durham: Duke University Press.

Brownmiller, S. (1975). *Against our will: Men, women, and rape.* New York: Simon & Schuster.

Chapman, J.R., and Bates, M. (1978). The victimization of women. Beverly Hills: Sage Publications.

Clark, L., and Lewis, D. (1977). *Rape: The price of coercive sexuality.* Toronto: Women's Press.

Estrich, S. (1987). *Real rape: How the legal system victimizes women who say no.* Cambridge, MA: Harvard University Press.

Finkelhor, D., and Yllo, K. (1985). *License to rape: Sexual abuse of wives*. New York: Holt, Rinehart, and Winston.

Gordon, M.T., and Riger, S. (1989). *The female fear*. New York: The Free Press.

Grossman, R., and Sutherland, J. (Eds.) (1982). *Surviving sexual assault*. New York: Congdon and Weed, Inc.

Groth, A.N., and Birnbaum, H.J. (1979). *Men who rape: The psychology of the offender, patterns of rape*. New York: Plenum Press.

Haskell, M. (1987). *From reverence to rape: The treatment of women in the movies* (2nd ed.). Chicago: University of Chicago Press.

Hazelwood, R.R., and Burgess, A.W. (1987). *Practical aspects of rape investigation: A multidisciplinary approach*. New York: Elsevier.

Hopkins, J. (Ed.) (1984). *Perspectives on rape and sexual assault*. London: Harper & Row.

Johnson, K.M. (1985). *If you are raped: What every woman needs to know*. Holmes Beach, FL: Learning Publications, Inc.

Katz, J.H. (1984). *No fairy godmothers, no magic wands: The healing process after rape*. Saratoga, CA: R & E Publishers.

Katz, S., and Mazur, M.A. (1979). *Understanding the rape victim: A synthesis of research findings*. New York: John Wiley & Sons.

Kelley, L. (1988). *Surviving sexual violence*. Minneapolis, MN: University of Minnesota Press.

Koss, M., and Harvey, M. (1987). *The rape victim: Clinical and community approaches to treatment*. Lexington, MA: The Stephen Greene Press.

LaFree, G.D. (1989). *Rape and criminal justice: The social construction of sexual assault.* Belmont, CA: Wadsworth Publishing Co.

McCahill, T.W., Meyer, L.C., and Fischman, A.M. (1979). *The aftermath of rape.* Lexington, MA: Lexington Books.

McEvoy, A.W., and Brookings, J.B. (1991) (2nd Ed.). *If she is raped: A Guidebook for husbands, fathers and male friends.* Holmes Beach, FL: Learning Publications.

Medea, A., and Thompton, K. (1974). *Against rape: A survival manual for women.* New York: Farrar, Straus, & Giroux.

Parrot, A. (1988). *Coping with date rape and acquaintance rape.* New York: The Rosen Publishing Group.

Parrot, A., and Bechhofer, L. (Eds.) (1990). *Acquaintance Rape: The hidden crime.* New York: John Wiley & Sons.

Pirog-Good, M.A., and Stets, J.E. (Eds.) (1989). *Violence in dating relationships: Emerging social issues.* New York: Praeger.

Pritchard, C. (1985). *Avoiding rape on and off campus.* Wenonah, NY: State College Publishing Company.

Roberts, C. (1989). *Women and rape.* New York: Harvester Wheat Sheaf.

Rowland, J. (1985). *The ultimate violation.* New York: Doubleday and Company, Inc.

Russell, D.E.H. (1975). *The politics of rape: The victim's perspective.* New York: Steen & Day.

Russell, D.E.H. (1984). *Sexual exploitation: Rape, child sexual abuse, and workplace harassment.* Beverly Hills, CA: Sage Publications.

Sanders, W.B. (1974). *Rape and women's identity.* Beverly Hills, CA: Sage Publications.

Storaska, F. (1975). *How to say no to a rapist and survive.* New York, NY: Random House.

Warner, C.G. (1980). *Rape and sexual assault - management and intervention.* London: Aspen Publications.

Warshaw, R. (1988). *I never called it rape: The Ms. report on recognizing, fighting, and surviving date and acquaintance rape.* New York: Harper and Row.

Webster, L. (Ed.) (1989). *Sexual assault and child sexual abuse: A national directory of victim/survivor services and prevention programs.* Phoenix, AZ: Oryx Press.

Williams, J.E., and Holmes, K.A. (1981). *The second assault: Rape and public attitudes.* Westport, CT: Greenwood Press.

SCHOLARLY ARTICLES AND PAPERS

Acquaintance Rape

Belkhap, J. (1988). "The sexual victimization of unmarried women by nonrelative acquaintances." In M. Pirog-Good & J. Stets, (Eds.), *Violence in dating.* Praeger.

Burkhart, B.R., and Stanton, A.L. (1985). "Sexual aggression in acquaintance relationships." In G. Russell (Ed.), *Violence in Intimate Relationships.* Englewood Cliffs, NJ: Spectrum.

Ellis, D. (1989). "Male abuse of a married or cohabitating female partner: The application of sociological theory to research findings." *Violence and Victims*, 4, 235-255.

Freund, K., and Blanchard, R. (1986). "The concept of courtship disorder." *Journal of Sex & Marital Therapy*, 12(2), 79-91.

Kanin, E.J. (1984). "Date rape: Unofficial criminals and victims." *Victimology: An International Journal*, 9(1), 95-108.

Koss, M.P.; Dinero, T.E.; and Seibel, C.A. (1988). "Stranger and acquaintance rape: Are there differences in the victim's experience?" *Psychology of Women's Quarterly*, 12, 1-24.

Lundberg-Love, P., and Geffner, R. (1988). "Date rape: Prevalence, risk factors, and a proposed model." In M. Pirog-Good & J. Stets, (Eds.), *Violence in dating*. Praeger.

Mandoki, C.A., and Burkhart, B.R. (1989). "Sexual victimization: Is there a vicious cycle?" *Violence and Victims*, 4, 179-190.

Muehlenhard, C.L., and Linton, M.A. (1985). *Sexual coercion in dating situations*. Paper presented at the annual meeting of the Association for Advancement of Behavior Therapy, Houston, TX.

Parrot, A. (1987, April). *University policies and procedures regarding acquaintance rape*. Paper presented at the Eastern regional meeting of the Society for the Scientific Study of Sex, Philadelphia, PA.

Parrot, A. (1987, November). *Using improvisational theater effectively in acquaintance rape prevention programs on college campuses*. Paper presented at the annual meeting of the Society of the Scientific Study of Sex, Atlanta, GA.

Parrot, A., and Allen, S. (1984, April). *Acquaintance rape: Seduction or crime? When sex becomes a crime*. Paper presented at the Eastern regional meeting of the Society for the Scientific Study of Sex, Philadelphia, PA.

Riggs, D.S.; O'Leary, K.D.; and Breslin, F.C. (1990). "Multiple correlates of physical aggression in dating couples." *Journal of Interpersonal Violence*, 5, 61-73.

Shotland, R.L. (1985). "A preliminary model of some causes of date rape. Special issue: Gender Roles." *Academy Psychology Bulletin*, 7(2), 187-200.

Shotland, R.L. (in press). "A model of the causes of date rape in developing and close relationships." In C. Hendrick (Ed.), *Review of Personality and Social Psychology*, Vol. 10. Sage.

Yegidis, B.L. (1986). "Date rape and other forced sexual encounters among college students." *Journal of Sex Education & Therapy*, 12(2), 51-54.

Zellman, G.L.; Goodchilds, J.D.; Johnson, P.B.; and Giarrusso, R. (1981, August). *Teenagers' application of the label "rape" to nonconsensual sex between acquaintances*. Paper presented at the meeting of the American Psychological Association, Los Angeles, CA.

Aftermath of Rape

Becker, J.V.; Skinner, L.J.; Abel, G.G.; and Cichon, J. (1986). "Level of postassault sexual functioning in rape and incest victims." *Archives of Sexual Behavior*, 15(1), 37-49.

Breslin, F.C.; Riggs, D.C.; O'Leary, K.D.; and Arias, I. (1990). "Family precursors: Expected and actual consequences of dating aggression." *Journal of Interpersonal Violence*, 5, 247-258.

Burgess, A.W., and Holmstrom, L.L. (1974). "Rape trauma syndrome." *American Journal of Psychiatry*, 131, 981-986.

Burgess, A.W., and Holmstrom, L.L. (1979). "Adaptive strategies and recovery from rape." *American Journal of Psychiatry*, 136, 1278-1282.

Burt, M., and Katz, B. (1987). "Dimensions of recovery from rape: Focus on growth outcomes." *Journal of Interpersonal Violence*, 2, 57-82.

Calhoun, K.S.; Atkeson, B.M.; and Resick, B.M. (1982). "A longitudinal examination of fear reactions in victims of rape." *Journal of Counseling Psychology*, 29(6), 655-661.

Calhoun, L.; Cann, A.; Selby, J.; and Magee, D. (1981). "Victim emotional response: Effects on social reaction to victims of rape." *British Journal of Social Psychology*, 11, 212-230.

Ellis, E.M., (1983). "A review of empirical rape research: Victim reactions and response to treatment." *Clinical Psychology Review*, 3, 473-490.

Frazier, P.A. (1990). "Victim attributions and post-rape trauma." *Journal of Personality and Social Psychology*, 59, 298-304.

Gidycz, C.A., and Koss, M.P. (1989). "The impact of adolescent sexual victimization: Standardized measures of anxiety, depression, and behavioral deviancy." *Violence and Victims*, 139-149.

Hamberger, L.K., and Arnold, J. (1989). "Dangerous distinctions among "abuse," "courtship violence," and "battering": A response to Rouse, Breen, and Howell." *Journal of Interpersonal Violence*, 4, 520-522. Rouse, L.P. (1989). "Reply to Hamberger and Arnold." *Journal of Interpersonal Violence*, 4, 523-527.

Kilpatrick, D.G.; Resick, P.A.; and Veronen, L.J. (1981). Effects of a rape experience — a longitudinal study. Journal of Social Issues, 37(4), 105-122.

Koss, M., and Burkhart, B. (1969),. "A conceptual analysis of rape victimization: Long-term effects and implications for treatment." *Psychology of Women Quarterly*, 13, 27-40.

Murnen, S.; Byrne, D.; and Perot, A. (1989). "Coping with unwanted sexual activity: Normative responses, situational determinants, and individual differences." *Journal of Sex Research*, 26, 85-106.

Myers, M.B.; Templer, D.I.; and Brown, R. (1984). "Coping ability of women who become victims of rape." *Journal of Consulting and Clinical Psychology*, 52(1), 73-78.

Parrot, A. (1986, June). *Emotional impact of acquaintance rape on college women*. Paper presented at the Midcontinent regional meeting of the Society for the Scientific Study of Sex, Madison, WI.

Rogers, L.C. (1985). "Sexual victimization in dating relationships: Effects on the social-psychological adjustment of college women." *Dissertation Abstracts International*, 45(9-B), 3081-3082.

Rynd, N. (1988). "Incidence of psychometric symptoms in rape victims." *The Journal of Sex Research*, 24, 155-161.

Stewart, B.D.; Hughes, C.; Frank, E.; Anderson, B.; Kendall, K.; and West, D. (1987). "The aftermath of rape: Profiles of immediate and delayed treatment seekers." *The Journal of Nervous and Mental Disease*, 175(2), 90-94.

Attitudes Toward Rape

Barber, R. (1974). "Judge and jury attitudes to rape." *Australian and New Zealand Journal of Criminology*, 7, 157-171.

Barnett, N.J., and Feild, H.S. (1977). "Sex differences in university students' attitudes toward rape." *Journal of College Students Personnel*, 18, 93-96.

Check, J.V.P., and Malamuth, N.M. (1983). "Sex role stereotyping and reactions to depictions of stranger versus acquaintance rape." *Journal of Personality and Social Psychology*, 45, 344-356.

Costin, F. (1985). "Beliefs about rape and women's social roles." *Archives of Sexual Behavior*, 14, 319-325.

Costin, F., and Schwartz, N. (1987). "Beliefs about rape and women's roles: A four-nation study." *Journal of Interpersonal Violence*, 2, 46-56.

Dull, R.T., and Giacopassi, D.J. (1987). "Demographic correlates of sexual and dating attitudes: A study of date rape." *Criminal Justice and Behavior*, 14(2), 175-193.

Feild, H.S. (1978). "Attitudes toward rape: A comparative analysis of police, rapists, crisis counselors, and citizens." *Journal of Personality and Social Psychology*, 36, 156-179.

Fischer, G.J. (1987). "Hispanic and majority student attitudes toward forcible date rape as a function of differences in attitudes toward women." *Sex Roles*, 17(1-2), 93-101.

Goodchilds, J.D.; Zellman, G.; Johnson, P.B.; and Giarrusso, R. (1988). "Adolescents and the Perceptions of Sexual Interactions." In A.W. Burgess (Ed.), *Sexual Assault*, Vol. II. New York: Garland Publishing Company.

Hall, E.R. (1987). "Adolescents' perceptions of sexual assault." *Journal of Sex Education and Therapy*, 13(1), 37-42.

Hall, E.R.; Howard, J.A.; Boezio, S.H.; and Boezio, L. (1986). "Tolerance of rape: A sexist or antisocial attitude?" *Psychology of Women Quarterly*, 10, 101-118.

Johnson, J.D., and Jackson, L.A. (1988). "Assessing the effects of factors that might underlie the differential perception of acquaintance and stranger rape." *Sex Roles*, 19(1-2), 37-45.

Kleinke, C.L., and Meyer, C. (1990). "Evaluation of rape victims by men and women with high and low belief in a just world." *Psychology of Women Quarterly*, 14, 343-353.

Kikuchi, J.J. (1988, April). *What do adolescents know and think about sexual abuse?* A paper presented at the National Symposium on Child Victimization, Anaheim, CA.

Korman, S.K., and Leslie, G.R. (1982). "The relationship of feminist ideology and date expense sharing to perceptions of sexual aggression in dating." *The Journal of Sex Research*, 18(2), 114-129.

L'Armand, K., and Pepitone, A. (1982). "Judgments of rape: A study of victim-rapist relationship and victim sexual history." *Personality and Social Psychology Bulletin*, 8, 134-139.

Larson, K., and Long, E. (1988). "Attitudes toward rape." *Journal of Sex Research*, 24, 299-304.

Malovich, N.J., and Stake, J.E. (1990). "Sexual harassment on campus: Individual differences in attitudes and beliefs." *Psychology of Women Quarterly*, 14, 63-81.

McKinney, K. (1986). "Perceptions of courtship violence: Gender difference and involvement." *Free Inquiry in Creative Sociology*, 14(1), 61-66.

Muehlenhard, C.L. (1983, December). *Sexual aggression in dating situation: Do factors that cause men to regard it as more justifiable also make it more probable?* Paper presented at the annual meeting of the Association for Advancement of Behavior Therapy, Washington, D.C.

Muehlenhard, C.L.; Friedman, D.E.; and Thomas, C.M. (1985). Is date rape justifiable? "The effects of dating activity, who initiated, who paid, and men's attitudes toward women." *Psychology of Women Quarterly*, 9(3), 297-310.

Quackenbush, R.L. (1980). A comparison of androgynous, masculine sex-typed, and undifferentiated males in dimensions of attitudes toward rape. Journal of Research in Personality, 23, 318-342.

Schultz, L.G., and DeSavage, J. (1975). "Rape and rape attitudes on a college campus." In L.G. Schultz (Ed.), *Rape victimology* (pp. 77-90). Springfield, Illinois: Charles C. Thomas.

Shotland, R.L., and Goodstein, L. (1983). "Just because she doesn't want to doesn't mean it's rape: An experimentally based causal model of the perception of rape in a dating situation." *Social Psychology Quarterly*, 46(3), 220-232.

Smith, M.J. (1985). "Sex role stereotypes and acquaintance rape: A study of rape attitudes." *Dissertation Abstracts International*, 45(8-B), 2702.

Tetreault, P.A., and Barnett, M.A. (1987). "Reactions to stranger and acquaintance rape." *Psychology of Women Quarterly*, 11, 353-358.

Attitudes Toward Rape Victims

Amick, A.E. (1986). "Perceptions of victim nonconsent to sexual aggression in dating situations: The effect of onset and type of protest." *Dissertation Abstracts International*, 46(7-B), 2451.

Borgida, E., and White, P. (1978). "Social perceptions of rape victims: The impact of legal reforms." *Law and Human Behavior*, 2, 339-351.

Deitz, S.R.; Blackwell, K.T.; Daley, P.C.; and Bentley, B.J. (1982). "Measurement of empathy toward rape victims and rapists." *Journal of Personality and Social Psychology*, 43, 372-384.

Gerdes, E.P.; Dammann, E.J.; and Heilig, K.E. (1988). "Perceptions of rape victims and assailants: Effects of physical attractiveness, acquaintance, and subject gender." *Sex Roles*, 19(3-4), 141-153.

Giacopassi, D.J., and Wilkinson, K.R. (1985). "Rape and the devalued victim." *Law and Human Behavior*, 9(4), 367-383.

Krulewitz, J.E. (1981). "Sex differences in evaluations of female and male victims' responses to assault." *Journal of Applied Social Psychology*, 11, 460-474.

Krulewitz, J.E. (1982). "Reactions to rape victims: Effects of rape circumstances, victim's emotional response, and sex of helper." *Journal of Counseling Psychology*, 29(6), 645-654.

Muehlenhard, C.L., and MacNaughton, J.S. (1988). "Women's beliefs about women who 'lead men on'." *Journal of Social and Clinical Psychology*, 7(1), 65-79.

Attribution of Responsibility

Acock, A.C., and Ireland, N.K. (1983). "Attribution of blame in rape cases: The impact of norm violation, gender, and sex-role attitude." *Sex Roles*, 9, 179-193.

Bridges, J.S., and McGrail, C.A. (1989). "Attributions of responsibility for date and stranger rape." *Sex Roles*, 21(3/4), 273-286.

Calhoun, L.G.; Selby, J.W.; and Warring, L.J. (1976). "Social perception of the victim's causal role in rape: An exploratory examination of four factors." *Human Relations*, 29(6), 517-526.

Cann, A.; Calhoun, L.G.; and Selby, J.W. (1979). "Attributing responsibility to the victim of rape: Influence of information regarding past sexual experience." *Human Relations*, 32, 57-67.

Coller, S.A., and Resick, P.A. (1987). "Women's attributions of responsibility for date rape: The influence of empathy and sex-role stereotyping." *Violence & Victims*, 2(2), 115-125.

Faust, S.K. (1986). "Knowledge of rape, self-esteem, and gender-basis of blame for friends of rape victims." *Dissertation Abstracts International, A: The Humanities and Social Sciences*, 47(1), 126.

Fenstermaker, S. (1988). "Acquaintance rape on campus: Attributions of responsibility and crime." In M. Pirog-Good & J. Stets, (Eds.), *Violence in dating*. Praeger.

Ferguson, P.A.; Duthie, D.A.; and Graf, R.G. (1987). "Attribution of responsibility to rapist and victim: The influence of victim's attractiveness and rape-related information." *Journal of Interpersonal Violence*, 2(3), 243-250.

Gilmartin-Zena, P. (1983). "Attribution theory and rape victim responsibility." *Deviant Behavior*, 4, 357-374.

Goodchilds, J.D.; Zellman, G.; Johnson, P.B.; and Giarrusso, R. (1979, April). *Adolescent perceptions of responsibility for dating outcomes*. A paper presented at the meeting of the Eastern Psychological Association, Philadelphia, PA.

Howard, J.A. (1984). "Societal influences on attribution: Blaming some victims more than others." *Journal of Personality and Social Psychology*, 47, 494-505.

Jacobsen, M.B., and Popovich, P.M. (1983). "Victim attractiveness and perceptions of responsibility in an ambiguous rape case." *Psychology of Women Quarterly*, 8(1), 100-104.

Jenkins, M.J., and Dambrot, F.H. (1987). "The attribution of date rape: Observer's attitudes and sexual experiences and the dating situation." *Journal of Applied Social Psychology*, 17(10), 875-895.

Kanekar, S., and Kolsawalla, M.B. (1980). "Responsibility of a rape victim due to her respectability, attractiveness, and provocativeness." *Journal of Social Psychology*, 112, 153-154.

Krahe, B. (1988). "Victim and observer characteristics as determinants of responsibility to victims of rape." *Journal of Applied Social Psychology*, 18(1), 50-58.

Krulewitz, J.E., and Payne, E.J. (1978). "Attributions about rape: Effects of rapist force, observer sex and sex role attitudes." *Journal of Applied Social Psychology*, 8, 291-305.

Pugh, M.D. (1983). "Contributory fault and rape convictions: Loglinear models for blaming the victim." *Social Psychology Quarterly*, 46, 233-242.

Richardson, D., and Campbell, J.L. (1982). "The effect of alcohol on attribution of blame for rape." *Personality and Social Psychology Bulletin*, 8, 468-476.

Sharp, J.A. (1987). *Date rape effects of victim/assailant intoxication, observer gender, and sex role stereotyping on attributions of responsibility*. Unpublished master's thesis, University of Kansas.

Smith, R.E., Keating, J.P., Hester, R.K., and Mitchell, H.E. (1976). "Role of justice considerations in the attribution of responsibility to a rape victim." *Journal of Research in Personality*, 10, 346-357.

Thornton, B.; Robbins, M.A.; and Johnson, J.A. (1981). "Social perception of the rape victim's culpability: The influence of respondent's personal-environmental causal attribution tendencies." *Human Relations*, 34, 225-237.

Thornton, B., and Ryckman, R.M. (1983). "The influence of a rape victim's physical attractiveness on observer's attribution of responsibility." *Human Relations*, 36(6), 549-562.

Thornton, B., and Ryckman, R.M., Robbins, M.A. (1982). "The relationships of observer characteristics to beliefs in the causal responsibility of victims of sexual assault." *Human Relations*, 35, 321-330.

Wilcox, P.L., and Jackson, T.T. (1985). "Fact variation: A study of responsibility versus fault." *Psychological Reports*, 56, 787-790.

Avoidance and Prevention

Atkeson, B.M.; Calhoun, K.S.; and Morris, K.T. (1989). "Victim resistance to rape: The relationship of previous victimization, demographics, and situational factors." *Archives of Sexual Behavior*, 18, 497-507.

Borden, L.A.; Karr, S.K.; and Caldwell-Colbert, A.I. (1988). "Effects of a university rape prevention program on attitudes and empathy toward rape." *Journal of College Student Development*, 29(2), 132-138.

Fischer, G.J. (1987). "College student attitudes toward forcible date rape: Changes after taking a human sexuality course." *Journal of Sex Education and Therapy*, 12(1), 42-46.

Furby, L.; Fischhoff, B.; and Morgan, M. (1989). "Judged effectiveness of common rape prevention and self-defense strategies." *Journal of Interpersonal Violence*, 4, 44-64.

Hazzard, A.P.; Kleemeier, C.P.; and Webb, C. (1990). "Teacher versus expert presentation of sexual abuse prevention programs." *Journal of Interpersonal Violence*, 5, 23-36.

Lee, L. (1987). "Rape prevention: Experiential training for men." *Journal of Counseling and Development*, 6, 100-101.

Levine-MacCombie, J., and Koss, M.P. (1986). "Acquaintance rape: Effective avoidance strategies." *Psychology of Women Quarterly*, 10(4), 311-319.

Parrot, A. (1989). "Acquaintance rape among adolescents: Identifying risk groups, and intervention strategies." *Journal of Social Work and Human Sexuality*, 8, 47-61.

Parrot, A. (1988, November). *Evaluating the effectiveness of an interdisciplinary model for acquaintance rape prevention for high school students*. Paper presented at the annual meeting of the Society for the Scientific Study of Sex, San Francisco, CA.

Quinsey, V.L., and Upfold, D. (1985). "Rape completion and victim injury as a function of female resistance strategy." *Canadian Journal of Behavioral Science*, 17, 40-49.

Riger, S., and Gordon, M. (1979). "The structure of rape prevention beliefs." *Personality and Social Psychology Bulletin,* 5, 186-190.

Roark, M.L. (1987). "Preventing violence on college campuses." *Journal of Counseling and Development,* 65(7), 367-371.

Sandberg, G.; Jackson, T.L.; and Petretic-Jackson, P. (1987). "College students' attitudes regarding sexual coercion and aggression: Developing educational and preventive strategies." *Journal of College Student Personnel,* 28(4), 302-311.

Youn, G. (1987). "On using public media for prevention of rape." *Psychological Reports,* 61, 237-238.

Developmental Antecedents to Sexual Aggression

Fagot, B.I.; Loeber, R.; and Reid, J.B. (1988). "Developmental determinants of male-to-female aggression." In G.W. Russell (Ed.), *Violence in Intimate Relationships.* New York: PMA Publishers.

Gwartney-Gibbs, P.A.; Stockard, J.; and Bohmer, S. (1987). "Learning courtship aggression: The influence of parents, peers, and personal experiences." *Family Relations: Journal of Applied Family & Child Studies,* 36(3), 276-282.

Perry, D.G.; Perry, L.C.; and Weiss, R.J. (1989). "Sex differences in the consequences that children anticipate for aggression." *Developmental Psychology,* 25(2), 1-8.

Incidence and Prevalence of Sexual Aggression

Aizenman, M., and Kelley, G. (1988). "The incidence of violence and acquaintance rape in dating relationships among college men and women." *Journal of College Student Development,* 29(4), 305-311.

Berger, R.J.; Searles, P.; Salem, R.G.; and Pierce, B. (1986). "Sexual assault in a college community." *Sociological Focus*, 19(1), 1-26.

Brodbelt, S. (1983). "College dating and aggression." *College Student Journal*, 17, 273-277.

Burkhart, B. (1983, December). *Acquaintance rape statistics and prevention*. Paper presented at the Acquaintance Rape and Prevention on Campus Conference in Louisville, KY.

Burnam, M.A.; Stein, J.A.; Golding, J.M.; Siegel, J.M.; Sorenson, S.B.; Forsythe, A.B.; and Telles, C.A. (1988). "Sexual assault and mental disorders in a community population." *Journal of Consulting and Clinical Psychology*, 56, 843-850.

Kirkpatrick, C., and Kanin, E.J. (1957). "Male sexual aggression on a university campus." *American Sociological Review*, 22, 52-58.

Koss, M.P.; Gidycz, C.A.; and Wisniewski, N. (1987). "The scope of rape: Incidence and prevalence of sexual aggression and victimizations in a national sample of higher education students." *Journal of Consulting and Clinical Psychology*, 55(2), 162-170.

Levine, E.M., and Kanin, E.J. (1987). "Sexual violence among dates and acquaintances: Trends and their implications for marriage and family." *Journal of Family Violence*, 2(1), 55-65.

Miller, B., and Marshall, J.C. (1987). "Coercive sex on the university campus." *Journal of College Student Personnel*, 28(1), 38-47.

Muehlenhard, C.L., and Linton, M.A. (1987). "Date rape and sexual aggression in dating situations: Incidence and risk factors." *Journal of Counseling Psychology*, 34(2), 186-196.

Parrot, A. (1985, November). *Comparison of acquaintance rape patterns among college students in a large co-ed university and a small women's college*. Paper presented at the annual meeting of the Society for the Scientific Study of Sex, San Diego, CA.

Parrot, A., and Link, R. (1983, April). *Acquaintance rape in a college population*. Paper presented at the Eastern regional Meeting of the Society for the Scientific Study of Sex, Philadelphia, PA.

Rivera, G.F., and Regoli, R.M. (1987). "Sexual victimization experiences of sorority women." *Sociology and Social Research*, 72, 39-42.

Sorenson, S.B.; Stein, J.A.; Siegel, J.M.; Golding, J.M.; and Burnam, M.A. (1987). "The prevalence of adult sexual assault: The Los Angeles Epidemiologic catchment area project." *American Journal of Epidemiology*, 126(6), 1154-1164.

Russell, D.E.H. (1982). "The prevalence and incidence of rape and attempted rape of females." *Victimology*, 7, 81-93.

Instruments and Scales

Koss, M., and Gidycz, C. (1985). "Sexual experiences survey: Reliability and validity." *Journal of Consulting and Clinical Psychology*, 53(3), 422-423.

Koss, M.P., and Oros, C.J. (1982). "Sexual experiences survey: A research instrument investigating sexual aggression and victimization." *Journal of Consulting and Clinical Psychology*, 50(3), 455-457.

Malamuth, N.M. (1989). "The attraction to sexual aggression scale: Part one." *Journal of Sex Research*, 26, 26-49.

Malamuth, N.M. (1989). "The attraction to sexual aggression scale: Part two." *Journal of Sex Research*, 26, 324-354.

Spence, J.T., and Helmreich, R. (1972). "The attitudes toward women scale: An objective instrument to measure attitudes toward the rights and roles of women in contemporary society." *JSAS Catalog of Selected Documents in Psychology*, 2, 1-48.

Ward, C. (1988). "The attitudes toward rape victims scale." *Psychology of Women Quarterly*, 12, 127-146.

The Male Victim of Sexual Aggression

Calderwood, D. (1987, May). "The male rape victim." *Medical Aspects of Human Sexuality*, 53-55.

Forman, B. (1982). "Reported male rape." *Victimology: An International Journal*, 7, 235-236.

Masters, W.H. (1986). "Sexual dysfunction as an aftermath of sexual assault of men by women." *Journal of Sex & Marital Therapy*, 12(1), 35-45.

Muehlenhard, C.L., and Cook, S.C. (1988). "Men's self-reports of unwanted sexual activity." *The Journal of Sex Research*, 24, 58-72.

Musialowski, D.M., and Kelley, K. (1987, April). *Male rape: Perception of the act and the victim*. Paper presented at the Eastern regional meeting of the Society for the Scientific Study of Sex, Philadelphia, PA.

Smith, R.E.; Pine, C.J.; and Hawley, M.E. (1988). "Social cognitions about adult male victims of female sexual assault." *The Journal of Sex Research*, 24, 101-112.

Struckman-Johnson, C. (1988). "Forced sex on dates: It happens to men, too." *The Journal of Sex Research*, 24, 234-241.

Miscommunication and Other Dating Dynamics Contributing to Rape

Abbey, A. (1982). "Sex differences in attributions for friendly behavior: Do males misperceive females' friendliness?" *Journal of Personality and Social Psychology*, 42, 830-838.

Abbey, A. (1987). "Misperceptions of friendly behaviors as sexual interest: A survey of naturally occurring incidents." *Psychology of Women Quarterly*, 11, 173-194.

Abbey, A., and Melby, C. (1986). "The effects of nonverbal cues on gender differences in perceptions of sexual intent." *Sex Roles*, 15(5/6), 283-288.

Allgeier, E.R. (1987). "Coercive versus consensual sexual interactions." *G. Stanley Hall Lecture Series*, Vol. 7 (pp. 7-63). Washington, D.C.: American Psychological Association.

Belk, S., and Snell, W. (1988). "Avoidance strategy use in intimate relationships." *Journal of Social and Clinical Psychology*, 7, 80-96.

Bushman, B.J., and Cooper, H.M. (1990). "Effects of alcohol on human aggression: An integrative research review." *Psychological Bulletin*, 107, 341-354.

Byers, E.S. (1988). "Effects of sexual arousal on men's and women's behavior in sexual disagreement situations." *The Journal of Sex Research*, 25(2), 235-254.

Byers, E.S., and Heinlein, L. (1989). "Predicting initiations and refusals of sexual activities in married and cohabitating couples." *The Journal of Sex Research*, 26, 210-231.

Byers, E.S., and Lewis, K. (1988). "Dating couples' disagreements over the desired level of sexual intimacy." *The Journal of Sex Research*, 24, 15-59.

Byers, E.S., and Wilson, P. (1985). "Accuracy of women's expectations regarding men's responses to refusals of sexual advances in dating situations." *International Journal of Women's Studies*, 8, 376-387.

George, W.H.; Gournic, S.J.; and McAfee, M.P. (1988). "Perceptions of post-drinking female sexuality: Effects of gender, beverage choice, and drink payment." *Journal of Applied Social Psychology*, 18, 1295-1317.

Giarrusso, R.; Johnson, P.; Goodchilds, J.; and Zellman, G. (1979, April). *Adolescent cues and signals: Sex and assault*. A paper presented at a Symposium of the Western Psychology Association meeting, San Diego, CA.

Goodchilds, J.D., and Zellman, G.L. (1984). "Sexual signaling and sexual aggression in adolescent relationships." In N.M. Malamuth and E. Donnerstein (Eds.), *Pornography and Sexual Aggression* (pp. 234-243). Orlando: Academic Press.

Harnish, R.J.; Abbey, A.; and Debono, K.G. (1989, April). *Misperceptions of friendliness cues: The effects of gender, physical attractiveness, personality similarity, and self-monitoring*. Paper presented at the annual meeting of the Eastern Psychological Association, Boston, MA.

Kelly, J.A.; Kern, J.M.; Kirkley, B.G.; and Patterson, J.N. (1980). "Reactions to assertive versus unassertive behavior: Differential effects for males and females and implications for assertiveness training." *Behavior Therapy*, 11, 670-682.

Knox, D., and Wilson, K. (1981). "Dating behaviors of university students." *Family Relations*, 30, 255-258.

LaPlante, M.N.; McCormick, N.; and Brannigan, G.G. (1980). "Living the sexual script: College students' views of influence in sexual encounters." *The Journal of Sex Research*, 16, 338-355.

Lewin, M. (1985). "Unwanted intercourse. The difficulty of saying no." *Psychology of Women Quarterly*, 9, 184-192.

Margolin, L. (1989). "Gender and the prerogatives of dating and marriage: An experimental assessment of a sample of college students." *Sex Roles*, 20(1/2), 91-102.

Margolin, L.; Miller, M.; and Moran, P.B. (1989). "When a kiss is not just a kiss: Relating violations of consent in kissing to rape myth acceptance." *Sex Roles*, 20(5/6), 231-243.

Margolin, L.; Moran, P.B.; and Miller, M. (1989). "Social approval for violations of sexual consent in marriage and dating." *Violence and Victims*, 4(1), 45-55.

Muehlenhard, C.L. (1988). "Misinterpreted dating behaviors and the risk of date rape." *Journal of Social and Clinical Psychology*, 6(1), 20-37.

Muehlenhard, C.L., and Andrews, S.L. (1985, November). *Open communication about sex: Will it reduce risk factors related to date rape?* Paper presented at the annual meeting of the Association for Advancement of Behavior Therapy, Houston, TX.

Muehlenhard, C.L.; Koralewski, M.A.; Andrews, S.L.; and Burdick, C.A. (1986). "Verbal and nonverbal cues that convey interest in dating: Two studies." *Behavior Therapy*, 17, 404-419.

Muehlenhard, C.L., and Hollabaugh, L.C. (1988). "Do women sometimes say no when they mean yes? The prevalence and correlates of women's token resistance to sex." *Journal of Personality and Social Psychology*, 54(5), 872-879.

Muehlenhard, C.L., and Long, P.L. (1988, November). *Men's and women's experiences of coercive sexual intercourse: How are they pressured and how do they react?* Paper presented at the annual meeting of the Society for the Scientific Study of Sex, San Francisco, CA.

Muehlenhard, C.L., and McFall, R.M. (1981). Dating initiation from a woman's perspective. Behavior Therapy, 12, 682-691.

Muehlenhard, C.L., and Scardino, T.J. (1985). "What will he think? Men's impressions of women who initiate dates and achieve academically." *Journal of Counseling Psychology*, 32, 560-659.

Peplau, L.A. (1984). "Power in dating relationships." In J. Freeman (Ed.), *Women: A feminist perspective* (pp. 100-112). Palo Alto, CA: Mayfield.

Ryan, K.M. (1988). "Rape and seduction scripts." *Psychology of Women Quarterly*, 12(2), 237-245.

Shotland, R.L., and Craig, J.M. (1988). "Can men and women differentiate between friendly and sexually interested behavior." *Social Psychology Quarterly*, 51(1), 66-73.

Snelling, H.A. (1975). "What is non-consent (in rape)?" In L.G. Schultz (Ed.), *Rape victimology* (pp. 157-163). Springfield, Illinois: Charles C. Thomas.

Struckman-Johnson, C., and Struckman-Johnson, D. (1988, November). *Strategies to obtain sex from unwilling dating partners: Incidence and acceptability.* Paper presented at the annual meeting of the Society for the Scientific Study of Sex, San Francisco, CA.

Zellman, G.L.; Johnson, P.B.; Giarrusso, R.; and Goodchilds, J.D. (1979, September). *Adolescent expectations for dating relationships: Consensus and conflict between the sexes.* Paper presented at the meetings of the American Psychological Association, New York, NY.

Profile of Sexually Coercive Males

Briere, M., and Malamuth, N.M. (1983). "Self-reported likelihood of sexual aggression: Attitudinal versus sexual explanations." *Journal of Research in Personality*, 17, 315-323.

Greendlinger, V., and Byrne, D. (1987). "Coercive sexual fantasies of college males as predictors of self-reported likelihood to rape and over sexual aggression." *Journal of Sex Research*, 23, 1-11.

Holmstrom, L.L., and Burgess, A.W. (1980). "Sexual behavior of assailants during reported rapes." *Archives of Sexual Behavior*, 9(5), 427-439.

Kanin, E.J. (1957). "Male aggression in dating-courtship relations." *American Journal of Sociology*, 63, 197-204.

Kanin, E.J. (1983). "Rape as a function of relative sexual frustration." *Psychological Reports*, 52, 133-134.

Kanin, E.J. (1985). "Date rapists: Differential sexual socialization and relative deprivation." *Archives of Sexual Behavior*, 14(3), 218-232.

Koss, M.P., and Leonard, K.E. (1984). "Sexually aggressive men: A review of empirical findings." In N. Malamuth & E. Donnerstein (Eds.), *Pornography and sexual aggression*, (pp. 213-232). New York: Academic Press.

Koss, M.P.; Leonard, K.E.; and Beezley, D.A. (1985). "Nonstranger sexual aggression: A discriminant analysis of the psychological characteristics of undetected offenders." *Sex Roles*, 12(9/10), 981-992.

Lipton, D.N.; McDonel, E.C.; and McFall, R.M. (1987). "Heterosocial perception in rapists." *Journal of Consulting and Clinical Psychology*, 55(1), 17-21.

Lisak, D., and Roth, S. (1988). "Motivational factors in nonincarcerated sexually aggressive men." *Journal of Personality and Social Psychology*, 55, 795-802.

Mahoney, E.R.; Shively, M.D.; and Traw, M. (1986). "Sexual coercion & assault: Male socialization and female risk." *Sexual Coercion & Assault*, 1(1), 2-8.

Malamuth, N.M. (1981). "Rape proclivity among males." *Journal of Social Issues*, 37, 138-157.

Malamuth, N.M. (1986). "Predictors of naturalistic sexual aggression." *Journal of Personality and Social Psychology*, 50(5), 953-962.

Malamuth, N.M.; Check, J.V.P.; and Briere, J. (1986). "Sexual arousal in response to aggression: Ideological, aggressive and sexual correlates." *Journal of Personality and Social Psychology*, 50, 330-340.

McKinney, K. (1986). "Measures of verbal, physical and sexual violence by gender." Free Inquiry in *Creative Sociology*, 14(1), 55-60.

Mosher, D.L., and Anderson, R.D. (1986). "Macho personality, sexual aggression, and reactions to guided imagery of realistic rape." *Journal of Research in Personality*, 20(1), 77-94.

Mosher, D.L., and Sirkin, M. (1984). "Measuring a macho personality constellation." *Journal of Research in Personality*, 18, 150-163.

Murphy, W.P.; Coleman, E.M.; and Haynes, M.R. (1986). "Factors related to coercive sexual behavior in a nonclinical samples of males." *Violence and Victims*, 1, 255-278.

Peterson, S.A., and Franzese, B. (1987). "Correlates of college men's sexual abuse of women." *Journal of College Student Personnel*, 28(3), 223-228.

Poppen, P.J., and Segal, N.J. (1988). "The influence of sex and sex role orientation on sexual coercion." *Sex Roles*, 19(11/12), 701.

Rapaport, K., and Burkhart, B. (1984). "Personality and attitudinal characteristics of sexually coercive college males." *Journal of Abnormal Psychology*, 93(2), 216-221.

Scott, R.L., and Tetreault, L.A. (1987). "Attitudes of rapists and other violent offenders toward women." *The Journal of Social Psychology*, 127(4), 375-380.

Scully, D., and Marolla, J. (1984). "Convicted rapists' vocabulary of motive: Excuses and justifications." *Social Problems*, 31, 530-544.

Scully, D., and Marolla, J. (1985). "Riding the bull at Gilley's: Convicted rapists describe the rewards of rape." *Social Problems*, 32(3), 251-263.

Tieger, T. (1981). "Self-rated likelihood of raping and the social perception of rape." *Journal of Research in Personality*, 15, 147-158.

Profile of Female Victims of Sexual Aggression

Amick, A.E., and Calhoun, K.S. (1987). "Resistance to sexual aggression: Personality, attitudinal, and situational factors." *Archives of Sexual Behavior*, 16(2), 153-163.

Bart, P.B. (1981). "A study of women who both were raped and avoided rape." *Journal of Social Issues*, 37(4), 123-137.

Burnett, R.C.; Templer, D.I.; and Barker, P.C. (1985). "Personality variables and circumstances of sexual assault predictive of a woman's resistance." *Archives of Sexual Behavior*, 14(2), 183-188.

Kanin, E.J. (1983). "Female rape fantasies: A victimization study." *Victimology: An International Journal*, 7(1-4), 114-121.

Kanin, E.J., and Parcell, S.R. (1977). "Sexual aggression: A second look at the offended female." *Archives of Sexual Behavior*, 6, 67-76.

Koss, M. (1985). "The hidden rape victim: Personality, attitudinal, and situational characteristics." *Psychology of Women Quarterly*, 9, 193-212.

Koss, M.P., and Dinero, T.E. (1989). "Discriminant analysis of risk factors for sexual victimization among a national sample of college women." *Journal of Consulting and Clinical Psychology*, 57, 242-250.

Selkin, J. (1978). "Protecting personal space: Victim and resister reactions to assaultive rape." *Journal of Community Psychology*, 6, 263-268.

Simkins, L.; Tarwater, K.; England, D.; and Roberts, M. (1986). *Predictors of sexual coercion by men and victimization experiences and coping styles of women.* Paper presented at the annual meeting of the Society of the Scientific Study of Sex, St. Louis, MI.

Skelton, C.A., and Burkhart, B.R. (1980). *Sexual assault: Determinants of victim disclosure. Criminal Justice and Behavior,* 7(2), 229-236.

Smeaton, G., and Byrne, D. (1987). "The effects of R-rated violence and erotica, individual differences, and victim characteristics on acquaintance rape proclivity." *Journal of Research in Personality,* 21, 171-184.

Wilson, W., and Durrenberger, R. (1982). "Comparison of rape and attempted rape victims." *Psychological Reports,* 50, 198.

Rape Myths

Briere, J.; Malamuth, N.M.; and Check, J.V.P. (1985). "Sexuality and rape-supportive beliefs." *International Journal of Women's Studies,* 8, 398-403.

Burt, M.R. (1980). "Cultural myths and supports for rape." *Journal of Personality and Social Psychology,* 38, 217-230.

Burt, M.R., and Albin, R.S. (1981). "Rape myths, rape definitions and probability of conviction." *Journal of Applied Social Psychology,* 11, 212-230.

Giacopassi, D.J., and Dull, R.T. (1986). "Gender and racial differences in the acceptance of rape myths within a college population." *Sex Roles,* 15(1/2), 63-75.

Malamuth, N.M., and Check, J.V.P. (1985). "The effects of aggressive pornography on beliefs in rape myths: Individual differences." *Journal of Research in Personality,* 19, 299-320.

Margolin, L. (1990). "Gender and the stolen kiss: Social support of male and female to violate a partner's sexual consent in a noncoercive situation." *Archives of Sexual Behavior*, 19, 281-292.

Schwendinger, J., and Schwendinger, H. (1974). "Rape myths: In legal, theoretical, and everyday practice." *Crime and Social Issues*, 1, 18-26.

Socio-Cultural Theories of Rape

Check, J.V.P., and Malamuth, N. (1985). "An empirical assessment of some feminist hypotheses about rape." *International Journal of Women's Studies*, 8, 414-423.

Ellis, L., and Beattie, C. (1983). "The feminist explanation for rape: An empirical test." *The Journal of Sex Research*, 19(1), 74-93.

Jackson, S. (1978). "The social context of rape: Sexual scripts and motivation." *Women's Studies International Quarterly*, 1, 27-38.

Jaffee, D., and Strauss, M.A. (1987). "Sexual climate and reported rape: A state-level analysis." *Archives of Sexual Behavior*, 16(2), 107-123.

Klemmack, S.H., and Klemmack, D.L. (1976). "The social definition of rape." In M.J. Walker and S.L. Brodsky (Eds.), *Sexual Assault* (pp. 135-147). Lexington, MA: D.C. Heath & Company.

Ploughman, P., and Stensrud, J. (1986). "The ecology of rape victimization: A case study of Buffalo, New York." *Genetic, Social, and General Psychology Monographs*, 112(3), 303-324.

Rose, V.M. (1977). "Rape as a social problem: A byproduct of the feminist movement." *Social Problems*, 25, 735-89.

Rozee-Koker, P.D. (1987). "Cross-cultural codes on seven types of rape." *Behavior Science Research*, 101-117.

Sanday, P.R. (1981). "The socio-cultural context of rape: A cross-cultural study." *Journal of Social Issues*, 37(4), 5-27.

Smith, M.D., & Bennett, N. (1985). "Poverty, inequality, and theories of forcible rape." *Crime and Delinquency*, 31(2), 295-305.

Williams, J. (1979). "Sex role stereotypes, women's liberation and rape: A cross-cultural analysis of attitudes." *Sociological Symposium*, 25, 61-97.